Intenti(

The science of creating the life you want

Hayley

*With Very best Wishes
to a great teacher and
mindfulness practitioner
Best Wishes*

Juliet

July 2019

INTENTIONAL
CREATIONS

Juliet Adams

St Johns Innovation Centre, Cambridge CB4 OWS
www.intentionalcreations.today

Front cover design: Hubspot_Pro
Copy Editor: Annie Jenkinson, Just Copyeditors.

Paperback: ISBN 978-1-9160844-0-7

Acknowledgements

This book is dedicated to my friend and colleague, neuroscientist and author Dr Tamara Russell – who contributed content, ideas and boundless energy to this project.

I would like to give thanks to all the individuals who inspired and shaped the case studies.

I would also like to thank all those who informed and inspired me through their writing and research in the field of intention, mindfulness, and neuroscience: especially (in no particular order) Dawson Church, Lynne McTaggart, Barbel Mohr, Elisabeth Pacherie, Dr Rick Hanson, Professor Mark Williams, Dr Shauna Shapiro, Amishi Jha, Andy Hafenbrack, Dr Jeremy Hunter, and Dr Jutta Tobias.

Table of Contents

About This Book

> "Your intentions set the stage for
> what is possible."
>
> - Shauna Shapiro, 2006

Intention is a very powerful thing. Whether you realise it or not, it underpins your every action. Everyone uses intention at an instinctual, unconscious level.

Only in recent years have academics started to research the impact of intention and propose theories on how intention works.

However, while the transformative power of intention is freely available to everyone, there is still very little written on the subject that is evidence-informed, practical, and accessible to all.

This book is a practical, no-nonsense guide based on the latest research, written for intelligent people who want to equip themselves with the knowledge necessary to transform every aspect of their lives, rather than blindly following gurus.

Intention Matters provides you with practical guidance enabling you to consciously focus and direct your intention to get the things you most want from life.

Intention can make the seemingly impossible, possible. It can transform your wealth, career, relationships, and happiness.

In this book, intention is defined as: 'A deep, sincere desire underpinned by a belief that it is possible'.

Intention and goals are *not* the same thing, which is why many goals fail to achieve the desired results. You will find more about this in Chapter 1.

When you set an intention, your mind tasks your brain, setting in motion cognitive processes that make things happen in the real world. In Chapter 1, you will discover the I-AM model that describes this process in more depth.

My interest in intention grew out of my work as a leadership development and workplace productivity specialist. Since 2009, I have been pioneering the use of mindfulness in a workplace setting. Mindfulness training is underpinned by over 3500 research papers. It enhances attentional control, leading to improvements in self-management and performance.

Over the years, I have taught thousands of busy working professionals in companies ranging from FSTE 100 organisations to local authorities and NHS trusts.

According to Shauna Shapiro (Mechanisms of Mindfulness: 2006), three core elements underpin mindfulness: intention, attention, and attitude.

The more I thought about intention, the more I realised it underpins pretty much everything we do in life. Everyone can benefit from the power of intention, and the possibilities are absolutely limitless; intention is a resource freely available to everyone, as long as you know how to activate it.

When I first set out to write this book, I intended to deliver a weighty academic tome for business people, with a few practical application chapters. In dialogue with leaders, HR managers, mindfulness trainers, business consultants and coaches, I decided that a quick-to-read, pocket-sized book would best meet my readers' needs and this book was born.

In this book, you will find:

- What intention is and why it matters.
- The science of intention, including the I-AM model to explain how intentions are activated.
- A step-by-step guide to help you start working with intention, including the IDEA framework that breaks the process into four easy steps.
- Tools and techniques to help you identify and achieve your core intentions.
- Practical troubleshooting hints and tips.

I recommend you read this book sequentially, but feel free to dip in and out too—in which case, you will find the glossary of terms at the back of the book useful.

It's *my* intention that this book will be practical and accessible, and that you, the reader, will quickly start to benefit from harnessing the power of intention, and start to create the life you want.

Juliet Adams, July 2019

Part One

What is intention, and why does it matter?

Chapter 1

Things you need to know about intention

"That which we manifest is before us; we are the creators of our own destiny. Be it through intention or ignorance, our successes and our failures have been brought on by none other than ourselves."

- Garth Stein, The Art of Racing in the Rain

In this chapter:

- ❧ *What is intention?*
- ❧ *Why intention is more powerful than goals*
- ❧ *Mega, core and nested intentions*
- ❧ *Examples of people who achieved their intentions against the odds*
- ❧ *Benefits of living and working with intention.*

What is intention?

Many people associate the word *intent* with the meaning that underlies or sits behind what people do and say. It is the motivation or the "bigger why" driving and shaping thoughts, speech and actions. Yet intention can be much broader and, hence, is a tricky concept to define.

In order to work with and actively engage with intention, it's important to define what intention is and—as has been shown above—the application of it; therefore, the definition of intention can differ.

The word intention comes from the Latin, *intentitus*—"a stretching toward." Below are some other common definitions:

- The American Heritage dictionary defines it as "an aim that guides action."

- In the Cambridge Dictionary, it is "something that you want and plan to do."

- The Merriam Webster dictionary defines it as "a determination to act in a certain way."

- Leonard Laskow, physician and researcher, refers to it as "holding attention on a desired outcome— holding attention requires will, which is a persistent, focused desire."

Taking these definitions into account together with academic research findings and my personal and professional experience in many settings, my working definition of intention is as follows:

Intention is a deep, sincere desire, coupled with a belief that it's possible.

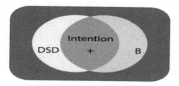

Figure 1: Intention = DSD +B. © 2019 Intentional Creations

The Intention Activation Model (I-AM) details how DSD +B activates the will (AW) and allocates attention (AA). This allows various cognitive processes in the brain networks (CP) to be harnessed, leading to actions, (A) turning intentions into reality (H).

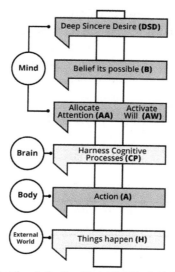

Figure 2: Intention Activation Model (I-AM). © 2019 Intentional Creations

The critical difference between goals and Intentions

From an early age at school, pupils are taught to set goals and work towards them. These goals must be SMART: specific, measurable, achievable, realistic, and time-bound. Whilst SMART goals might help you to get a school assignment in on time, meet a performance target at work or deliver a project, they can also be highly restrictive. Their tight focus is both a help and a limitation, depending on the circumstance—and the intention!

Goals keep you on track but often inhibit creativity and innovation. Sometimes, they turn out to be barriers to achieving what's really important or needed at work, at home or in life in general. In these times of uncertainty and volatility, goals may actually hamper your progress. Working with intention, conversely, allows you to be more flexible, agile and resilient. Intention is increasingly recognised as a cognitive skill that can be learned. Intentions are often confused with goals but there are a number of critical differences.

Goals	Mega, core and nested intentions
Future-focussed	Bigger and bolder! Rooted in the present moment
Narrow	Broad
A destination or specific achievement	Lived each day, independent of reaching the goal or destination
Usually short-term	Often longer-term
Usually fixed and logical	Creative and intuitive
Often externally imposed or superficial	Often heartfelt and personal, arising from a well deep within

Intention forms

Intentions and the scale of intentions vary from person to person. For the purpose of this book, I have split intentions into four categories: mega intentions, core intentions, nested intentions, and micro intentions.

The majority of Part Two of this book focusses on working with life-changing *core* intentions. If you are new to working with intention, day-changing micro intentions are a great place to start.

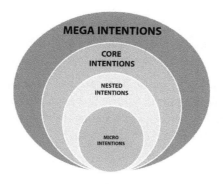

Figure 3: Different forms of intention. © 2019 Intentional Creations

> ✎ **Mega Intentions** – huge, potentially world-changing intentions. Mega intentions are not for the faint-hearted and may take a lifetime to achieve or even get started. If you surface a mega intention in Step 1 of the IDEA process, you will definitely need to break it down into core, nested and micro intentions. Failure to do this may lead to a sense of overwhelm, procrastination, fear and not getting started at all.

You will need to involve others to bring it to fruition.

- **Core intentions** – Smaller in scale and far more self-contained than mega intentions. May contribute to the achievement of mega intentions or stand alone.

- **Nested intentions** - Intentions that, when achieved, contribute to the achievement of your core intention. You might initially identify these as core intentions then later discover they form a part of a greater or overarching intention to which this intention contributes.

- **Micro intentions** – smaller in scale and duration than nested or core intentions. You might set an intention for the day or an intention for a meeting or important conversation. See Chapter 4 for more examples.

In Chapters 5 & 6, you will find details of a number of case studies on working with intention. These include Fernando and Advik (mega intentions), and Natasha, Helen and Hank (core and nested intentions).

The power of intention

Whether you realise it or not, intention already shapes many aspects of your life. Your conscious and unconscious intentions influence your choice of a life partner, your career, the way you raise your children, where you live, the car you drive, how much money you have; the list is endless.

Limiting beliefs (see Chapter 11) such as "I'll never be able to get that job" or "I'm not good enough or smart enough" narrow your field of vision and make you feel you have limited choices, but in reality, these limitations are largely self-imposed. History is littered with examples of people who achieved their intentions against the odds.

- **THOMAS EDISON** - one of the most prolific inventors in history, was homeschooled from the age of four because his school thought he was "too stupid to learn". His mother hid this from her son, teaching Thomas herself. Despite only receiving three months' formal schooling, his intention to be an inventor led to him becoming one of the most prolific inventors in history.

- **WALT DISNEY** – after visiting various amusement parks with his daughters in the 1930s and 1940s, he became determined to create Disneyland as a tourist attraction to entertain fans who wished to visit. Despite being turned down by over 100 banks when he tried to get funding to develop Disneyland, and suffering from several bankruptcies, he went on to achieve his intent. Disneyland now has a larger cumulative attendance than any other theme park in the world.

Would Edison or Disney have achieved the same success if they had let self-limiting beliefs or the beliefs of others get in the way? Firm, unwavering intention is what drove them forward to achieve what others deemed impossible.

More recent examples of career success fuelled by the power of intention include:

- Author **JK ROWLING** had the intention to write a book about a child who escaped the confines of the adult world and went off somewhere where he had power, both literally and metaphorically. She believed strongly that this was a book both children and adults would enjoy reading, and set an intention to write the book and get it published. She was a divorced single parent living on benefits when she wrote Harry Potter and the Philosopher's Stone. It took her seven years from idea to completed book. She was then rejected by twelve publishers before finally being published and becoming one of the most successful authors of all time.

- ❧ **HOWARD SCHULTZ** was inspired by Italian espresso cafes following a trip to Milan. He set an intention to upscale these cafes and introduce them across America. He pitched the idea to his Seattle-based coffee bean roaster employer, who had no interest whatsoever in owning coffee shops but agreed to finance Schultz's endeavour. They sold him their brand name, Starbucks, not expecting much to come of it. In 2018, Starbucks' net worth was estimated at $30bn.

The Intention of Rowling and Schultz led to the creation of products that touched the lives of billions of people worldwide.

Everyone can benefit from the power of intention, whatever their circumstance. Jean-Dominique Bauby, Eddie the Eagle, Ruby Wax, and Shona McKenzie—all dear friends of mine—are shining examples of what is possible.

- ❧ Well-loved actress and comedian **RUBY WAX** experienced episodes of depression for most of her life. When she finally checked into a clinic, she realised how widespread mental health problems were, forming a strong intention to do something to help others. In 2013, she gained her master's degree in mindfulness-based cognitive therapy from Oxford University. She worked with Comic Relief to start to reduce the taboos surrounding mental health, featuring on posters that read: "*One in four people have a mental illness, one in five people have dandruff, I have both.*" She took her illness on the road and got people talking honestly and openly about mental health. Her shows, TV and media interviews, and books have had a truly transformative effect on attitudes towards mental health around the world.

❧ At the age of forty-six, **JEAN-DOMINIQUE BAUBY**[1] was working as the editor-in-chief of French Elle magazine. In 1995, he suffered a massive stroke and lapsed into a coma. He awoke twenty days later, mentally aware of his surroundings, but paralysed and unable to speak. Despite this, he wrote the number-one best-selling book *The Diving Bell and the Butterfly*, later adapted to produce a multiple award-winning movie. The entire book was written by Bauby blinking his left eyelid, which took ten months, working for four hours each day. The book took about 200,000 blinks to write and an average word took approximately two minutes.

❧ Mum of two **SHONA McKENZIE**[2] developed depression and anxiety and an eating disorder when her husband walked out on her. She fell off a chair while painting her son's bedroom and broke her back in two places; she was diagnosed with osteoporosis. Doctors initially told her she would never walk again. Shona formed a strong intention to walk and get her life back on track, asking doctors to draw a diagram of exactly where the breaks were in her back. Each day, she meditated on the bone breaks with the intention that they would mend. In less than two months, she was walking again. Against the odds, her bone density increased. A year later, she qualified as a full-time fitness instructor.

The common themes flowing through all these success stories are intention and belief. If you are clear of your intention and have a strong belief that it is possible, the potential is limitless.

Why intention is more powerful than goals

Earlier in this chapter, I explained some of the reasons why goal-setting often fails to deliver the desired results. The Intention Activation Model (I-AM) explains this further.

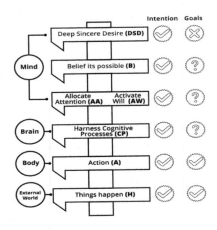

Figure 4: The Intention Activation Model (I-AM) illustrates why intent is more important than goals © 2019 Intentional Creations

The starting point for harnessing the power of intention is a Deep Sincere Desire (DSD); this is not usually the starting point for goals.

Belief (B) is required to ignite the conviction that things can be different. This is not always the case, particularly if goals are imposed.

Goals lead to partial or unstructured Activation of Will (AW) and the application of Focussed Attention (FA).

Assuming you really want to achieve the goal, and it hasn't been imposed on you by someone else, the goal should lead to actions, resulting in things happening.

This illustrates why goal-setting can be ineffective, as it fails to effectively stimulate the mind and brain to provide the energy to drive the machinery—both mental and physical—that makes things happen.

See Chapter 3 for a full explanation of the I-AM model.

The benefits of living and working with intention

Grasping the potential of working with intention provides you with three essential life skills:

- 🐾 It helps you manage your most important resource, attention.
- 🐾 It gives you greater choices in life.
- 🐾 It saves energy.

Intention saves time and energy

Setting a firm intention can be very helpful as it assists you to drop those things that are NOT in line with your intention.

Having set intentions, the cognitive processes of your brain can more easily work out when you have gone off track. This means you can drop what's not your priority or what is not important—or, in that moment, less important—and get back on track, saving energy and time.

At the mental level, if you set the intention to listen (for example), then you will more easily notice when you are *not* listening, perhaps because you are daydreaming, lost in a fantasy about a holiday, or rehearsing your reply. You are able to release from this mental activity more promptly and come back to just listening. By having the intention to listen, you will hear so much more, and more clearly.

Just listening—and minimising the associated mind-wandering—is effective because it means your brain can encode a deeper level of data in the listening process. You will remember more about what was said and have a greater memory of all the more subtle non-verbal information that contextualised what was said. It also feels completely different for the person you are listening to, thus deepening relationships and trust.

In today's world, this is so important as there are so many energy drainers and distractors for your mind and brain. If you never pause to stop and check in with your intentions, distractions can keep you endlessly busy for years, decades even.

Intention gives you more choices in life

One great thing about working with intention is that it gives you more choices. In that moment of awareness, when you realise you are not on track with your plan or intention, you have a choice; in fact, you have several. You can carry on with what you were doing—perhaps having a nice daydream or getting distracted again by social media—or you can choose to get back to your task. At this point, you can also—if you wish, and if it's necessary—modify your intentions.

Unlike goals which tend to be finite, thus leading to "success or failure", intentions have flexibility and can be revisited at any time.

Intention directs and turbo-charges attention

The act of setting an intention can harness the full power of your mind and brain to many tasks. Your attention becomes turbo charged when your mind allocates attention to the outcome you desire, triggering cognitive processes in your brain's attention network. You'll find more information on this in Chapter 2.

Let's unpack the example above, the intention to listen.

After deciding that listening is important and setting the intention to listen, your attentional system is primed to prioritise the auditory stream. Anything coming into your brain through your ears automatically has a "priority" VIP pass to your conscious awareness. In this way, intention focusses and guides attention.

When you notice you are thinking about emails you've left unanswered, whether or not the next client will be on time or that you forgot to buy toilet paper on your way home, the fact that you have set the intention to listen means your brain will quickly alert you to these non-VIP mental sensations all clamouring to get into the VIP lounge. If their names are not on the list, they are not coming in! The task of your brain is to quickly drop those thoughts and get back to giving priority to the auditory stream – the voice of the person you are listening to.

Two important things happen when an intention is set. Your brain is primed to attend to any sensations bearing stimulus properties in line with *what you expect on the basis of the intention* (e.g. a voice and the use of your ears). Secondly, you are promptly alerted when "not listening" arises, meaning you get back on track more quickly.

Summary

- An intention is 'A deep, sincere desire (for something to happen) underpinned by a belief that it is possible.

- Intentions fall into three main categories:

    - Micro intentions which may change your day

    - Core / nested intentions that can change your life

    - Mega intentions that may change the world.

- Goals and intentions are often confused but are very different. Goals fail to stimulate the mind and brain optimally, so tend to have less impact.

- ๑ Intention helps you to manage your attention, saving energy, and giving you greater choices in life.

- ๑ If you are clear on your intentions and have belief, the possibilities are limitless.

References

1. Information about Jean-Dominique Bauby can be found on Wikipedia: https://en.wikipedia.org/wiki/Jean-Dominique_Bauby

2. Article about Shona McKenzie: https://www.theguardian.com/lifeandstyle/2000/jul/11/healthandwellbeing.health1

Chapter 2

How intention impacts your mind, brain and body

"Your beliefs become your thoughts,
Your thoughts become your words,
Your words become your actions,
Your actions become your habits,
Your habits become your values,
Your values become your destiny."

– Mahatma Gandhi

In this chapter:

- ❧ *How abstract becomes concrete and thoughts become reality*

- ❧ *The relationship between your mind and brain*

- ❧ *Understanding the impact of intention on your mind, brain and body*

In this chapter, I will share with you some of the growing science behind intention. Intention drives attention, and there is certainly evidence that attention training (particularly with mindfulness) changes key regions of the brain that support cognition and emotion regulation[1].

There is also work showing how intentions "set up" the brain to help it connect with what it intends, and respond promptly when things are not going to plan.

You don't need to be a neuroscientist to understand this chapter, but I will introduce you to a few key brain regions. This knowledge will help you to know—at least to some degree— what you are doing with your brain when you start working with intention, and why the more you practice, the better it gets.

As you change your brain, so you begin to shape your life in different, more positive and healthy ways that fulfil you.

When you set an intention, your mind tasks your brain, and your brain tasks the limbs of your body to take action.

As explained in Chapter 1, intention is a *deep sincere desire, underpinned by a belief that it is possible,* activating your will and focussing your attention. This, in turn, harnesses various cognitive processes leading to actions that make things happen in the real world. In this way, an abstract idea or big dream moves from your mind, into your brain, through your body and then, finally, out into the world.

The abstract becomes concrete. Thoughts become reality.

The I-AM model, explained in more detail in Chapter 3, breaks down the elements that can turn a wish into a real-world event. The early stages of the process involve the mind and the brain.

In common speech and literature, the terms 'mind' and 'brain' are often used interchangeably, causing confusion. There is no single universally-agreed definition of 'mind'. The next few pages will help you to understand the key practical and philosophical debates on the difference between the mind and brain, and cast some light on how they work together, along with working definitions for the purpose of this book.

The mind vs. brain debate

How your mind shapes your reality, and the way in which your brain supports your body to act in and on the world are topics mystifying thinkers throughout human history. Even today, with all the scientific studies and advances in neuroscience, there is still confusion.

As this is a practical book, I will not attempt to review or resolve these issues; however, it is important for you—the reader—to understand my position in relation to the mind-brain issue.

What scientists do agree on, is that your mind, your conscious experience of the world around you (the environment) impacts on your brain. What has been learned over the last few decades of neuroscience research is that the brain has a greater ability to adapt and develop in adulthood than previously thought. The brain's ability to adapt and develop is called neuroplasticity; more about this later in this chapter.

As a result, your brain is constantly changing and evolving. To use a well-worn phrase, you *can* teach an old dog new tricks, good news for all of us!

Mind	Brain
Not physical	Physical hardware (it occupies space in your skull.)
Turns chemical / electrical impulses into mental experiences (images or thoughts)	Transmits information via chemical impulses.
Uses the information gathered to enable you to become consciously aware of the world and your experiences, thoughts and feelings	Gathers information via your five senses, linking it to existing information stored in your brain. Stores and retrieves information.
Possesses a sixth sense—introspection, (exploring what you are thinking or feeling), which is not specifically linked to one area of your brain.	Has five distinct regions dedicated to processing incoming information from each of your five senses.
Is capable of mental time-travel (remembering things that happened in the past, planning or anticipating your future)	Can only operate in the present moment
Master.	Servant
Interprets and shapes your reality via thoughts and feelings Tasks your brain (directs voluntary thoughts, speech and action)	Receives commands from your mind. Is activated or engaged by your mind.

The mind – a definition

There is no single, universally-agreed definition of 'the mind'. According to the Oxford dictionary, the mind is "the element of a person that enables them to be aware of the world and their experiences, to think, and to feel; the faculty of consciousness and thought."

For the purposes of this book, *mind* refers to the unlimited creative force utilising the brain to make things happen. Think of the common language of the mind. You might say "I changed my mind" or "I haven't yet made my mind up." These phrases give a clue to the malleable and subjective nature of *mind*.

You can literally have anything in your mind—even things that don't exist or aren't real—like a horse with the head of a cow or roller-skates instead of hooves. Your mind also has an amazing capacity to time-travel to the past or the future. It can remember things that have already happened and simulate or imagine scenarios that have not yet happened, and may or may not occur. The mind is not limited by time.

The mind aids the brain, enabling consciousness, perception, thinking, judgment, and memory.

The brain – a definition

Your brain is an organ located within the skull, which receives, organises, and distributes information. It can be thought of as 'hardware' or to use a more technical phrase, the "wetware" of your conscious experience.

Your brain is made up of neurons, glia, blood vessels, fluid-filled ventricles and other structures which, when working in harmony, provide us with a functioning body and an experience of *being conscious*. The brain is the centre of all functions, and without the brain, it is impossible to survive.

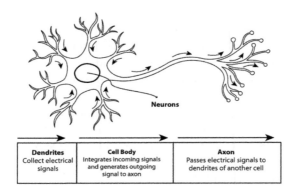

Figure 5: How information flows through the neurons in your brain

Understanding some basics on how the brain works will help you to understand and work with intention. The next few pages provide you with an executive overview.

Left and right hemispheres

The brain has two halves or hemispheres, left and right, which seem to have some common and some distinct functions. Broadly speaking, the left hemisphere undertakes functions that require categorization, a narrowing of the attentional field, concrete reasoning, and many language functions.

At the cellular level, the left hemisphere has a small number of densely-connected hubs, with many long-range connections. In contrast, the right hemisphere is a bit messier. There are more nodes, less densely connected and over shorter distances. It is thought that the right hemisphere is more about getting the "gist" of things. It is involved in understanding metaphors, processing emotions and bodily sensations. It is sometimes referred to as the creative or emotional side of the brain.

The three brain systems

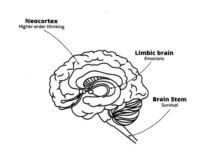

It can be helpful to think of the brain as having three key systems. Although this is an over-simplification, it provides an easy model to work with. These three areas of the brain do not work in isolation; they work together, one area acting as the driver of the other areas.

Figure 6: The three brain systems.

At the base of the brain is the **'brain stem'**—a set of structures that take care of your basic survival functions, such as breathing and digestion, blood pressure, and heart rate.

Above this can be found a set of structures called **the Limbic system**, responsible for your emotional responses, including your fight or flight survival response.

Both the brain stem and the limbic system control your behaviour at a core and instinctual level. These areas of the brain are very fast, energy efficient, and operate mostly at an unconscious level.

The **neocortex,** regarded by some as the newest part of the brain, is far more flexible in the way it processes information and is orientated towards the achievement of tasks, goals and conscious intentions. When you need to plan, prioritise, make decisions, or come up with new ideas, you engage this area of the brain. In comparison to the brain stem and limbic system, the neocortex is slow and energy hungry. As a result, in a drive for efficiency, the brain will frequently find ways to automate. This creates habits stored in the lower areas of the brain, freeing up the neocortex for tasks requiring thinking, planning and creativity.

This is not always beneficial, as people often default to patterns of thinking and behaviour that are no longer relevant or helpful.

Neuroplasticity

Contrary to popular thought, your brain is not fixed and unchangeable when you reach adulthood; it is constantly being shaped by experience. With every repetition of a thought or emotion, you reinforce a neural pathway, and with each new thought, you begin to create a new way of being. These small changes, frequently enough repeated, lead to changes in how your brain works.

Over time, new ways of thinking and behaving become automatic, a part of you. You literally become what you think and do. Neuroplasticity plays a major role in setting intentions which make things happen in the real world.

The neuroscience of intention

Elisabeth Pacherie's work has conceptualised two different levels of intention. Whilst some intentions are "proximal" (close in time), others are distal (further away in time). Micro intentions are proximal, while nested, core and mega intentions are distal. The moment you intend for something to happen, the brain forms a powerful *motor representation* (MR).

MR is the mental precursor of action and is normally conscious. Unconscious MR can get converted into conscious MR, resulting in motor imagery (MI). MI is a mental process allowing the brain to rehearse what it wants to happen. MI provides you with an awareness of what is intended and a conscious awareness of the need for your body to take action to make things happen. For more on this, read the work of intention researcher, Elisabeth Pacherie[2].

The starting point for the Intention Activation Model (I-AM) described in Chapter 3 is the mind tasking the brain.

Whilst many think that your mind and brain guide your body, there is increasing evidence that your body has a considerable impact on your brain and mind. Researchers and clinicians are slowly catching up to ideas elaborated over millennia in the east—that the mind and body are fully interconnected and constantly impacting on one another.

Your heart sends far more signals to your brain than your brain sends to your heart. The heart is in a constant two-way dialogue with the brain. Your emotional state changes the signals the brain sends to the heart, and the heart responds in complex ways. Research shows that messages the heart sends the brain can profoundly affect your performance.

When you are excited or feel trepidation, you may experience a sensation often described as 'butterflies in your stomach'. This sensation is triggered by a network of neurones in your gut. This network is so extensive, scientists have nicknamed it 'the little brain'. The neurones in your gut do much more than merely handle digestion. In conjunction with your brain, the 100 million neurones of the little brain influence your emotions and determine your mental state.

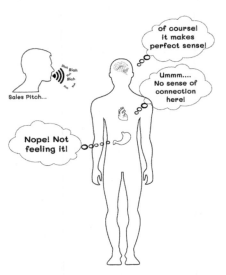

Figure 7: The mind: body connection. © 2019 Intentional Creations

Rather than just being a bunch of limbs dragged around by a busy brain, it is becoming clearer that the body has a different, more innate type of wisdom. Those that can tap into both the thinking brain and the feeling body will have a distinct advantage. The starting point of an intention is a deep, sincere desire. Tapping into the messages the body sends you will help you identify the things you really want, which may be very different from what society and peers think you should want. You will find more about this in Chapter 10.

Summary

- ﹌ In order for an intention to take shape in the real world, the mind must task the brain, making the abstract concrete and turning thoughts into reality.

- ﹌ Whilst the brain is physical, the mind is not. The mind acts as a master, while the brain acts as a humble servant.

- ﹌ The 'little brain' is located in your gut. It influences your emotions and shapes your emotional state.

- ﹌ In order to work effectively with intention, you need to harness the mind, brain and body.

- ﹌ Proximal and distal intentions trigger a powerful motor representation in the brain, resulting in mental imagery which starts to convert intentions into reality.

References

1. Minds "At Attention": Mindfulness Training Curbs Attentional Lapses in Military Cohorts (2015) Amishi Jha

2. The content of intentions (2000) Elisabeth Pacherie

Chapter 3

The science of intention activation

" For the last 400 years, an unstated assumption of science is that human intention cannot affect what we call physical reality. Our experimental research of the past decade shows that, for today's world and under the right conditions, this assumption is no longer correct."

– William A. Tiller, Professor Emeritus, Stanford University[1]

In this chapter:

- *How intention works*
  - *Research into the neuroscience of intention*
  - *Research linking energy and intention*
- *How intention is activated*
  - *How your mind tasks your brain*
  - *How your brain triggers cognitive processes*

A huge volume of research highlights the important role that intention plays in transforming an idea, desire or wish into reality. How it does this is the subject of much debate.

Numerous research studies and most of the books and published works on intention to date are based on a certain presumption; this is that the act of setting an intention unleashes or generates an energy force that makes things happen. Whilst this may be the explanation, in this book, I offer a simpler one. I assert that intentions turn heartfelt wishes into reality as a result of a chain reaction in the mind, brain, and body.

Energy and intention

The methods I outline in this book to help you work with intention, are based on neuroscientific explanations of how intention works. For completeness, and to help you become a more informed reader, in the next few pages I have included details of the evidence linking energy and intention.

The Intention Experiment

In 'The Intention Experiment: Use Your Thoughts to Change the World' (2007), author Lynne McTaggart uses cutting-edge research conducted at Princeton, MIT, Stanford, and other universities and laboratories to reveal that intention is capable of profoundly affecting all aspects of life. She presents research that suggests thought generates its own palpable energy, which can be used for good or ill. McTaggart worked to distil the practice of persons such qigong masters, master healers, and Buddhist monks, discovering that they use common techniques, with many similarities.

Her research revealed that people who are really good at manifesting things with their thoughts do so because they are able to use the power of intention in a very sophisticated way.

She concludes that the most important thing when working with intention is first clearing the mind via a meditative state, and then achieving a deep and intense focus. Doing so brings about intention mastery, as opposed to wishful thinking. Hundreds of research studies demonstrate the effectiveness of mindfulness meditation as a tool to focus your attention. You will find more about this in Chapter 10.

The impact of intention on healing

Many believe that intention plays a major role in healing. There are many research studies published on the positive impact of prayer, energy-based healing such as Reiki, and the intention or belief of medical physicians and their patients.

These include robust research by Schmidt et al (2008)[2,3]. Schmidt's research: 'Can we help just by good intentions? A meta-analysis of experiments on distant intention effects' studied healing sent by healers to patients not in the same room as the healer. The research concluded that intention was common to all the healing methods studied, and "the intentional aspect [of the different forms of healing studied] is key.

Modern manifestation

In recent years, a number of best-selling books have offered guidance on how you can develop the ability to manifest or create the things you want in your life. Intention is a core component of manifesting. A number of these books suggest that intention taps into universal energy, and/or by 'asking the universe' you will get the outcomes you seek.

In her 1997 book, *The Cosmic Ordering Service,* Bärbel Mohr proposes that you can order anything you desire from the cosmos. It's based on the presumption that everything is interconnected and there's some kind of consciousness holding all the material world together. Critics describe this as "a type of positive thinking" or "goal setting wrapped up in spiritual language".

Mohr describes the underpinning principle as follows: "When you order with the cosmos, you connect yourself additionally with what others call 'united field theory' and others 'morphogenetic field' or 'Akasha Chronicle'. One assumes that basically everything is one and that you are able to connect with the power of the entirety." This book and its numerous spin-offs have been a bestseller for many years, and many people, including TV celebrity Noel Edmunds, testify that it changed their lives.

Rhonda Byrne's book *The Secret* (2006) and the sequel *The Power* (2010) are also based on the law of attraction. It's based on the ancient wisdom that "Like with like together strike".

If your thoughts are of wealth, then before you know it, you will receive wealth. Some describe *The Secret* as a form of mental hygiene. "It matters what you're thinking because thoughts are things. So to change your thoughts is to change things as they are in the world."

Critics say it's simply positive thinking, repackaged, or a "pop-psych version CBT (cognitive behavioural therapy). Like *The Cosmic Ordering Service, The Secret* has been a best seller for many years and has many devotees and advocates.

There are many books now published on the law of attraction and manifestation. The problem is that some of these pseudo-science-based books require the reader to have blind faith and belief in the process without explaining how or why it works. Having a strong belief in the outcome you desire certainly increases the chances of you connecting with opportunities that may be helpful, but it is not a guarantee.

In the writing of this book, I have striven to research the evidence base for intention from a brain-based perspective to give you, the reader an evidence-informed approach to working with intention that is practical, easy to understand and apply. At no point in this book do I ask you to apply blind faith or trust in a higher force to deliver your intention.

If asking God or a higher being or energy force helps you to work with intention, feel free to do so. The model of intention activation does not require blind faith or belief in a god or the power of the cosmos, as you will discover in the next few pages.

The Intention Activation Model (I-AM)

The Intention Activation Model (I-AM) describes, in simple terms, how your **mind** tasks your **brain** which guides your **body** to take **action** leading to **things happening** in the real world.

The next few pages explain this further by breaking down each element of the I-AM.

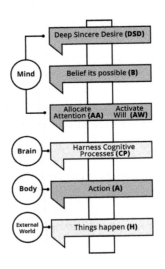

Figure 8: Intention Activation Model (I-AM). © 2019 Intentional Creations

How your mind tasks your brain

The I-AM breaks down the ingredients of intention, which, when combined in the right order, lead to a wish becoming a reality. It describes how the mind tasks the brain, which guides the body, leading to decisions and actions that make things happen in the real world.

In Chapter 2, I described the difference between the mind and brain. Whilst the brain is physical, the mind is not. The mind can be likened to the master, while the brain follows instructions. The mind is an unlimited creative force utilising the brain to make things happen.

The starting point of the I-AM model is the mind registering a genuine, heartfelt desire to make something happen, which— when coupled with a belief that it is possible—activates your will and allocates attention to the task. Many intentions fail because people wish for things they don't actually want, or don't believe are possible.

Intention starts with a deep, sincere desire

The starting point for working with intention is a desire for something to happen. In this I-AM model, this is called 'a deep, sincere, desire' or 'DSD' for short.

There is a big difference between everyday desires and DSD's. An example of an everyday desire might be "I want that coat" or "I want that sports car" or "I would like to be doing her (or his) job". You might momentarily want to buy that coat, shoes, suit or dress, but do you really want them, or is it a passing fancy? The same could be said of the car or the job; do you

37

really want the reality of owning that car, or doing that job day every day for the foreseeable future? Is it *you* that wants it, or is it societal or cultural pressure making you *think you want it?*

In contrast, a DSD is something you really want. A deep, sincere desire (DSD) is the bigger why. Why you are in that job? Why do you burn the midnight oil to do that research? Why do you spend your free time campaigning or volunteering? Why is it important that you parent your children in a certain way?

If you strip away peer or family pressure, societal norms and cultural expectations, your DSD's are the things YOU really want at a heartfelt level. Techniques to help you identify and refine your DSD's are discussed more deeply in Chapters 5-9.

The power of belief

Having identified your DSD's, you need to check your beliefs support your DSD's. If you have a DSD out of alignment with your beliefs, you are unlikely to achieve your intention. Similarly, if you have a DSD but unconsciously think it's unachievable, it's unlikely to happen.

Your beliefs essentially influence ninety-five percent of the decisions you make and the actions you take. They form the foundations of your self-concept, determining how you see yourself in relation to the world around you. The labels you give yourself, the limitations you put on yourself, and the expectations you have of yourself are all built upon your belief systems. If your belief systems are not aligned with your intentions or imposed goals, you will feel stuck, unfulfilled, and miserable. In Chapter 11, you will find techniques to help you to surface and work with your beliefs.

Activating your will and allocating your attention

Once you have identified your DSD's and feel confident that your beliefs support the achievement of your intentions, your mind gets to work. It activates your will and allocates your attention, in turn triggering a series of complex cognitive processes in your brain.

How your brain triggers cognitive processes

Intentions that start in your mind activate your will and focus your attention. In order for this intention and will to be expressed in the world, you need to harness various cognitive processes and engage the brain and body to make things happen in the world.

The majority of your cognitive processes take place at a subconscious level. You can consciously support your subconscious by taking simple actions that help you to hardwire any necessary changes into your brain and make any necessary life changes to help your intention take shape, grow and blossom.

The role of your conscious and unconscious mind in intention activation

Your conscious mind is like the conductor of an orchestra giving out orders. The orchestra—the subconscious and the deeper unconscious—carry out the orders. The conductor may be in charge of the orchestra but the orchestra plays the music.

The conscious mind communicates to the outside world

and the inner self through speech, pictures, writing, physical movement, and thought. The subconscious mind is in charge of your recent memories and in continuous contact with the resources of the unconscious mind.

The unconscious mind is the storehouse of all memories and past experiences. These memories and experiences shape your beliefs, habits, and behaviours. The unconscious constantly communicates with the conscious mind via your *sub*conscious. It helps you make sense and draw conclusions about your interactions with the world.

The vast majority of all brain activity occurs at a subconscious level. The cognitive processes underpinning the achievement of the I-AM model are largely unconscious. Key cognitive processes that underpin the achievement of intention include:

- Attention
- Default mode network
- Working memory
- Emotion regulation
- Reward circuits
- Habit formation.

In the next few pages, you will find a brief overview of each of the above, but first, it's important to understand a little about the conscious and subconscious activity of the mind.

Attention

Your brain's attention network is able to change and develop far more than was originally thought. Your attention network consists of a group of brain regions spanning the frontal and parietal (back and side) lobes.

The attention network allows you to move and shift your attention, change the aperture of your attentional lens, be aware when attention has been "captured" and make decisions about how and where to focus attention when you meet a conflict. When your attention network experiences something unexpected, novel, or dangerous, your anterior cingulate (a critical part of the attention network located in the frontal lobe) swings into action. It directs more attention to what is going on so you can solve the problem.

The role of your default mode network

The term "default mode" is used by neuroscientists to describe brain activity when there are no visual scenes to look at or mental tasks going on. The default mode network is an interconnected group of brain structures including the medial prefrontal cortex, posterior cingulate cortex, and the inferior parietal lobule, the lateral temporal cortex, and hippocampus.

The default mode network group of brain regions will show higher levels of activity when your mind is not engaged in specific, targeted thinking. It is during these times that your mind might be wandering—daydreaming, recalling memories, envisioning the future achievement of your intentions, monitoring the environment, and so on. These moments of mind wandering may result in eureka moments, such as new ideas, fresh perspectives and thematic thinking around your intention, all contributing to the achievement of your intentions.

Working memory

Working memory is a cognitive system responsible for temporarily holding information available for processing. It plays an important role in reasoning, decision-making and behaviour. Some neuroscientists believe that working memory allows you to work with information stored in your brain. Your working memory allows you to hold information "in mind" over a period of time.

You use your working memory for just about everything you do. It allows you to have a "workbench" in the mind of your intentions, as well as the sub-components necessary to allow your intentions to be met. Any task requiring you to bring up your intentions and memories and hold them "online" as you go about creating plans and tasks to meet your objectives, is using working memory.

Your working memory is required to help you to hold in mind the bigger picture and working objectives. Your intentions, once set, work in the background, to identify and tune into opportunities that "match" intentions. In addition, your working memory responds promptly to any mismatched experiences that will take you off track and away from your desired intentions. This helps you to strengthen this network and make it more efficient.

Your working memory is compromised when you get stressed. Under pressure, your attention allocation may receive conflicting demands. You may struggle to hold in mind everything you need to, and start to forget things. Mindfulness training can help you to manage your emotions and reduce the impact of stress on working memory. More about this in Chapter 10.

Emotion Regulation

Your emotional state can have a huge impact on your cognition. Many people pride themselves on their ability to deny, suppress and avoid outward displays of emotions. Research suggests that these strategies may not be as helpful as first thought.

It's impossible to make decisions in the absence of emotions Denying your emotional experience can have negative consequences on your mental and physical health[4]. Emotional suppression can mean that you lose access to a vast "data lake" of information that helps you make even more skilful and wise decisions.

Intending to attend to emotions, immediately turns the tables on your often automatic reaction to avoid negative emotions. In the avoidance, you surrender your will to the emotion. Its appearance is directing your mind, energy and actions.

Reward system and dopamine

The reward system refers to a group of structures activated whenever you experience something rewarding like eating chocolate, being praised or achieving a goal. The reward system of the brain is connected to brain areas controlling your behaviour and memory. When something rewarding is encountered, neurons release dopamine to make you feel pleasure. Areas of the brain areas impacted by pleasure include your amygdala and nucleus accumbens. Pleasure and reward will increase momentum towards your desired intention.

Habit formation

Habit formation is the process by which new behaviours become automatic. The behavioural patterns you repeat most often are etched into your neural pathways, and stored in an area of your brain called the basal ganglia. The basal ganglia are a group of subcortical nuclei situated at the base of the forebrain, and these are strongly interconnected with the cerebral cortex, thalamus, and brainstem, as well as several other brain areas.

In order to form a habit, you need three things: a context **cue**, behavioural repetition (**routine**), and the **reward**[5]. Let's look at forming a habit to take off your shoes as you enter the house. Your context might be arriving home, while your cue might be opening the front door. Your behaviour would be to bend down and take off your shoes and place them in the shoe rack. Your reward might be keeping the house clean or making your partner happy.

Habits may initially be triggered by a goal, but over time, that goal becomes less necessary and the habit more automatic. Developing helpful habits connected to your intentions will help you achieve your intent.

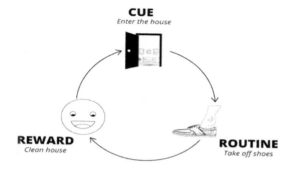

Figure 9: How habits are formed. © 2019 Intentional Creations

Using your body to take action

In the final step, you take action—passively or actively. When taking action, it's important to monitor and manage yourself to ensure you avoid putting yourself under excessive pressure [trying too hard!] since this will stop you from achieving your intent.

As I just mentioned, when taking action, monitoring and managing yourself are critical. Making an intention a reality can take time, and getting desperate or over-striving will activate primitive brain circuitry designed to keep you safe from harm. This reduces your ability to be creative and notice when opportunities arise that could help you achieve your intentions.

Noticing and taking advantage of arising opportunities will lead to you taking action—as and when the time is right. When opportunities arise, take them, don't obsess or worry about them; there is a much greater probability that your decision will be right than wrong.

In Chapter 9, you will find techniques to help you become more vigilant, looking out for opportunities that arise to help you towards your intention.

Making your intentions a reality

As a result of taking actions, things will start to happen for you in the 'real world'. It's important to notice and consciously celebrate all the small wins you have on the way to achieving your intentions.

Whilst over-analysis and excess thinking is to be avoided, it's important to get a sense that things are moving in the right direction, even if some of the pieces of the jigsaw puzzle are still missing.

If you are convinced you are moving in the wrong direction, use it as a learning opportunity. It's also worth revisiting the intention you set and checking if it's still right for you, or needs amending. Sometimes, by taking action and making things happen, you realise what you *don't want*, in turn helping you to become clearer about what you *do want*.

Summary

When you set an intention, your mind tasks your brain, which triggers cognitive processes helping you to achieve your intention. These processes include devoting attentional resources to the task in hand, utilising your working memory, tuning into your emotional responses, forming helpful habits, igniting your reward circuitry (so you gain a sense of pleasure and achievement when things start to happen), and forming new, helpful habits that assist you in making your intention a reality.

- ❧ A large volume of research highlights the important role intention plays in transforming an idea, desire or wish into reality.

- ❧ There are two key schools of thought on how intention turns your wishes or desires into reality:

  - ❧ Intentions take form as a result of tapping into a universal energy source or creating energy.

  - ❧ Intentions take form as a result of your mind tasking your brain and body. This is the area this book focusses on.

- ❧ The I-AM model describes how a deep, sincere desire coupled with a belief that it's possible activates will and allocates attention to the task of achieving the intention. This, in turn, triggers various cognitive processes in the brain, guiding your body to take action that leads to intentions becoming a reality

References

1. William A. Tiller, Professor Emeritus, Stanford University. Quoted in McTaggart, Lynne. The Intention Experiment: Use Your Thoughts to Change the World. Harper Element, 2007.

2. Cloninger, CR. (2007) Spirituality and the Science of Feeling Good. Southern Medical Journal.

3. Schmidt, SJ. (2012) Can we help just by good intentions? A meta-analysis of experiments on distant intention effects. Journal

of alternative and complementary medicine (New York, N.Y.) 18(6):529-33·

4. Mauss IB, Gross JJ. Emotion suppression and cardiovascular disease: Is hiding feelings bad for your heart? In: Nyklicek I, Temoshok L, Vingerhoets A, editors. Emotional expression and health: Advances in theory, assessment and clinical applications. New York: Brunner-Routledge; 2004. pp. 61–81

5. Wood, W., & Neal, D. T. (2016). Healthy through habit: Interventions for initiating & maintaining health behavior change. Behavioral Science & Policy.

Part Two

Working with intention

Part Two

Working with Families

Chapter 4

Changing your day with intentions

"Every moment of our lives, we are surrounded by an abundance of possibilities and have access to an infinity of choices."

– Juliet Adams

In this chapter:

- ❧ *How to set an intention that changes your day*

- ❧ *How to set a moment-changing intention with real impact*

- ❧ *Tools and techniques to help you start working with intentions*

Intention is a very powerful thing, underpinning your every action. You often use it at an instinctual unconscious level. When I set out to write this book, my initial focus was on the use of intention to change your life. About halfway through writing the book, however, I realised I was missing something fundamental.

Intentions do not always have to be life-changing. Do they?

It's equally important to have moment-changing or day-changing intentions. I describe these as 'micro intentions'. This title may be a little bit misleading. In comparison to a mega intention or core intention (see Chapter 1), a day- or moment-changing intention may seem tiny in size, but its impact can be huge.

Intentions have no limits. They are expansive and life-changing or much smaller in scale. You can set an intention for the world, your life, each day, or for a short moment of time. Setting intentions can make you more effective, and will open your eyes to things you may have otherwise missed.

Setting an intention for your day

When you set an intention for the day, you enter everything that happens that day with a new mindset—even if you were just walking into work, stuck in traffic, drinking coffee, or working. As an example, let's say you set an intention to nurture yourself that day. Your friend Joe asks you out to a club for a drink and some dancing after work. Your internal dialogue might be:

"If I say yes and go out for a drink, will it make me feel nurtured?"

"When I went for drinks with Joe last time, I ended up with a hangover next day. Do I want to feel that way tomorrow morning? I'll end up eating chicken and chips and blow my diet."

"Maybe going out for a drink isn't going to make me feel nurtured."

"Is there another way to spend time with Joe that feels more nurturing?"

"I think I'm going to choose to politely say no to clubbing for tonight and find a time later in the week when we can get tea and have a nice walk in the afternoon."

Your intention has become your inner GPS system, allowing you to make empowered decisions that align with your intention.

Setting an instant intention

Setting an instant intention can change your experience of many things you encounter daily. You can set an instant intention for your daily commute, for a meeting that's normally boring or unproductive, for an encounter with a friend or work colleague or for spending time with a loved one.

The list is endless, the possibilities limitless.

Case studies

Many people who set micro intentions for the first time are surprised by their impact.

The meeting

Tom attended a departmental meeting on the last Friday of every month at 10 p.m. – 12 p.m. It regularly overran, cutting his lunch break short. In previous meetings, Tom felt bored and frustrated and hated it when people talked over each other, didn't listen and acted with political self-interest. The meeting was chaired by a different departmental head each month, with the aim of spreading the workload fairly. This month was Tom's turn to be chair.

Tom set an intention that this time, it was going to be different. He set the intention that everyone would have the chance to be heard, no one would talk over anyone else, and the meeting would end on time.

With this intention loaded into his internal GPS, he chose to start the meeting differently, by summarising the purpose of the meeting and gaining agreement about what they wanted to achieve collectively in the next two hours. He then allocated everyone the same time each to present their ideas. No one was allowed to interrupt while they were presenting. He then gave everyone one minute to respond to what had been presented, one at a time. He summarised the feedback, an action was agreed and the meeting moved on to the next presenter. Tom was surprised when the meeting came to a natural end at 11.40 a.m.

If Tom had not set this intention, the chances are he would have walked into the meeting with a mindset that it was hopeless and a waste of time, and simply gritted his teeth and battled his way through. By setting an intention he sincerely wanted and believing it was possible for the meeting, transformed his thoughts about the meeting, setting in train cognitive processes and actions that fundamentally changed the meeting experience for everyone attending.

The teenage son

Ginny was a busy mum with two teenagers. Her eldest son was behaving like the BBC TV character 'Kevin the teenager'. He was stroppy, non-communicative, and everything was 'so unfair'! This coupled with her hectic life made conversations difficult and unpleasant, so at that moment in time, mother and son gave each other a wide berth.

At 5 p.m. as Ginny was just about to leave work, she received a call from her son's youth leader to say he had vanished from the after-school club, they did not know where he was and were concerned he might be involved in a gang. Ginny tried phoning her son but it kept going to voicemail. She panicked, dreading the conversation when he came home.

Commuting home, she had visions of him dropping out of college, getting involved in drugs and being stabbed in a gang war. Eventually, she realised she simply did not know and was only winding her self up with these doom-laden stories. She set an intention to set aside her thoughts and concerns and really listen to him with an open mind.

When she arrived home, her son was sitting in the living room with his best friend Simeon—a nice lad—playing on his PS4 game station. She asked Simeon to join them for something to eat. After eating, when Simeon had left, Ginny spoke to her son. She told him she had been called by his after school club

l what had happened. He said "Club was boring, so
to come home with Simeon so I could thrash him
playing Spiderman II."

She calmly asked him why he hadn't told anyone he was
leaving. He replied that he had tried but the youth leaders
were doing other things and they had been told to wait, and
he got bored of waiting and caught a bus with Simeon straight
home to avoid walking through the estate and getting caught
up with gang politics.

In this case study, it would have been easy for the conversation
to have turned into a blazing row achieving little and probably
making the situation worse. Ginny's intention steered her
through to a more helpful outcome.

Cultivating the good

Sonia had been reading Rick Hanson's excellent book
'Hardwiring Happiness'. She recognised the human negativity
bias meant that she (like most humans) tended to pay too
much attention to the bad things in life and too little to the
nice things passing her by unnoticed.

Following Rick's advice, she decided to set an intention for the
day to notice when nice things happened; and deliberately
pause for a couple of minutes so she could soak in the good
feelings. In this way she would consciously recognise that
something good had happened. She recognised that this small
action would start the process of hard-wiring happiness into
her brain.

Her intention led her to notice a beautiful sunrise as she left the house. She noticed how easily her car started and that the car kept her warm and dry despite the heavy rain outside. She gave thanks for quickly finding a parking space near the office. She noticed and appreciated the smile on the nice young man's face as he opened the door for her when she entered the office laden with bags and files.

She paused to appreciate the first cup of tea, freshly-brewed, steaming on her desk. The day went on in this manner. During that day, she also had a tough negotiation with a difficult client and was set a challenging deadline on a complex project she was working on. She also had a slow commute home due to an accident ahead. As she passed the accident, she gave thanks that it was not her, and the ambulance was on hand to help the injured driver.

Sonia's day had its challenges, but to her surprise, her intention for the day powerfully transformed her experience of it for the better.

A trip to IKEA

Mary-Jane had contracted Hank to fit a new kitchen, and a trip to IKEA was planned. Mary-Jane hated IKEA—the crowds, the enormity of the warehouse, the meatballs in the canteen, not to mention the queues in the car park. Mary-Jane was dreading it. Hank, on the other hand, saw it as a fun day and set an intention to have as much fun as possible and a great day out (he didn't get out often!).

On arriving at IKEA, they parked easily, much to Mary-Jane's surprise. Mary-Jane was on a mission to get in and get out quickly, wanting to quickly confirm her kitchen unit choices, choose accessories and finalise the plan so that the kitchen could be ordered. Hank, on the other hand, had different ideas. He wanted a coffee before embarking on the IKEA experience, so grudgingly, Mary-Jane followed him into the canteen and bought him a coffee, which then stretched to a cake each too. Mary-Jane marvelled at Hank's joy at having a cup of coffee in an IKEA mug overlooking the comings and goings in the IKEA car park.

Leaving the canteen, she started to walk at a pace through the showroom, heading for the kitchens area—about halfway around, following the prescribed IKEA route. She quickly noticed that Hank was lagging behind looking at everything in detail. He looked at the design, the colour, the utility and hidden uses for the goods on display with childlike curiosity and joy. She slowed her pace to watch him. He played with light switches, opened and shut boxes, and watched the human dynamics at play. Eventually, she started to join in the fun, playing with remote lighting controls when she reached the kitchen showrooms, then smiling inwardly when she made other customers jump when lights in cabinets suddenly dimmed or brightened on their approach.

Kitchen planning completed, units finalised and ordered, Hank announced it was time for lunch and chose a large plate of meatballs in cream sauce with lingonberry jelly and mash. Mary-Jane chose a salmon salad. After eating, they slowly walked through the Market Hall area, and Mary-Jane selected some new pans and drawer organisers. Hank treated himself to some new tea towels.

Reaching the car at 3 p.m., Mary-Jane marvelled at the fact she had spent five hours in IKEA and actually had quite a fun day. Hank's intention had not only transformed his day, but Mary-Jane's too. Hank is the subject of a case study, the outline of which you will find in Chapter 5.

Techniques to help you identify micro intentions

Before working on life-changing core or even mega intentions, it's best to start with some micro intentions.

Working with micro intentions tends to be simpler than core or mega intentions but the principles are the same.

Ways to identify day-changing intentions

As a reminder, an intention is "a deep sincere desire, underpinned by a belief that it is possible". Set aside the how and when and fine detail, just focussing on the thing you really want. Here are some ideas to get you started. Ask yourself one or more of the following questions:

- What do I really want today?

- What do I most need today?

- What do I most desire today?

- What one thing do I want to change today?

- What attitude do I want to adopt today?

- What would I like to really notice today?

- How can I best look after myself today?

∿ How can I be the best I can be today?

Use the answers gained as the basis for your intention for the day.

Ways to identify instant intentions

Pick something you would like to change or would like to be different.

If you are having a busy day and your head is in a whirl, mindfulness can help you to calm and settle yourself. When busy but wishing to set an intention, spend a short while narrowly focussing your attention. You could focus on the physical sensations of breathing, how your feet feel in contact with the floor, or focus on the loudness, softness and quality of a specific sound. If your mind wanders, gently bring it back. Do this for at least a minute, longer if you can, then ask yourself one or more of the following questions:

∿ How would I like the next two hours to be?

∿ How would I like the meeting to go?

∿ How would I like to be in this conversation?

∿ How would I like to feel this morning/afternoon/ evening?

∿ How brave or courageous do I want to be?

∿ What would I like others to take away from this?

∿ How can I make a difference right now?

Use the answers to help you form an instant intention.

Summary

- ❧ Intentions have no limits. They are expansive and life-changing or much smaller in scale.

- ❧ You can set an intention to change the world, your life, each day, or a short moment.

- ❧ Setting intentions can make you more effective, opening your eyes to things you may otherwise have missed.

- ❧ You can set an intention at any time to change the trajectory of your day.

- ❧ Micro intentions include both 'day-changing intentions' and 'instant' (moment-changing) intentions.

- ❧ Micro intentions can lead to rapid outcomes, making them a great place to start when working with intentions per se.

- ❧ Additional resources and case studies that support this chapter are available from my website: www.intention-matters.com

Chapter 5

Introducing the IDEA framework

" Have the courage to follow your heart and intuition. They somehow know what you truly want to become."

– Steve Jobs: Business magnate, Co-Founder of Apple INC.

In this chapter:

- ❧ *Assessing your readiness*

- ❧ *An overview of four simple steps to help you harness the power of intention*

- ❧ *Identifying and testing your beliefs*

- ❧ *Intention case studies.*

In Chapter 3, you gained an overview of the science that underpins intention, and the different theories about how and why intention works. The I-AM model provided a neuroscience-based explanation of how intention starts in the mind, which tasks the brain, leading to a series of cognitive processes that guide you to take action that makes your intention a reality.

In Chapter 4, you discovered how to use proximal intention to transform your day.

In this chapter, I introduce you to the IDEA framework, providing you with four steps to help you to start working with bigger nested, core or even hairy audacious mega intentions. The remaining chapters of Part Two provide detailed information and techniques to help you to work with distal intentions.

Whatever your intention, the four steps of the IDEA model will help you identify, refine and embody your intentions to transform your thoughts into real-world events, but first a word about rituals...

The role of ceremonies and rituals

Ceremonies and rituals form a core element of birthday celebrations, weddings and funerals. There are Christmas rituals, drinking rituals, and working rituals. Those who practice magic perform rituals to focus their intention to make something happen. Those who work as energy healers use symbols and rituals to focus intention in order to send healing energy to others. Sporting events often start with the ritual of playing or singing the national anthem, ending with ritual handshakes.

A number of researchers now link rituals with the achievement of outcomes[2,3]. Researchers Mike Norton and Francesca Gino[4] discovered that people who undertake rituals following a death reported a higher feeling of control and less grief regarding their loss. Simple rituals can be extremely effective. Rituals performed after experiencing losses alleviate grief. Rituals performed before high-pressure tasks—like public speaking or job interviews—reduce anxiety and increase people's confidence.

Intriguingly, even those who claim not to believe that rituals work still benefit from them. Rituals have a tangible impact on thoughts, feelings, and behaviours, leading to improved outcomes; they help you to focus and intensify your intentions.

Are rituals an essential part of working with intention? No.

Can they help you to work more successfully with intentions? Yes!

If rituals leave you cold, don't use them. They are offered in this book as an optional extra. Feel free to skip to the end of this chapter.

If rituals appeal to you, and you feel they add gravitas to the process, why not create your own? First, identify and distil your intentions, then make and use a ritual to help the embedding process. Rituals can be anything you like. The power of the ritual comes not from what you do, but from your brain's connection between the ritual and the desired outcome. Be creative and have fun. Here are some ideas:

- ❧ Find a quiet room. Place a candle in front of you. Light the candle and state your intention. Hold your intention in mind as you watch the candle flickering and dancing. Let go of your intention and trust that it will start to take shape as you blow the candle out.

- ❧ Find a small pebble or stone that you feel attracted to. Place the pebble in the palm of your hand. Bring to mind your intention. Slowly close your fingers carefully around the object. Visualise the outcome(s) of your intentions, pausing for a moment to let them unfold. Open your fingers and with your other hand, place the pebble somewhere you will see it regularly. The mantelpiece, your desk or on your bedside table might be good places. Each time you see the stone, it will remind you of your intention.

- ❧ Sit down and place your hands palm down on your lap. Tap your right hand three times on your right upper leg. As you do so, bring to mind your intention, as if it were happening here and now. Trust that it will unfold in the best way possible for you. Once a day at a chosen time, tap your right upper leg gently to re-affirm your intention.

Assessing readiness

Before getting started, it's worth checking in with yourself to test your readiness. There are points in everyone's life when the time is simply not right and circumstances may impede the process. They may include:

- ❧ Transitions points in life such as leaving home, moving

house, moving to another country, or changing your job.

❧ Becoming ill or disabled.

❧ Dealing with the death of family or close friends.

❧ Your children going to college or leaving home.

❧ The requirement to provide long-term care for a parent, child, or partner.

❧ Going through a divorce or the break-up of a long term relationship.

This list is not exhaustive, and may not prove to be a barrier to working with intention, but at times like this, you need to check in with yourself and see if the time is really right for you. If the answer is yes, by all means, proceed, but remember to be kind and patient with yourself and cut yourself some slack.

The IDEA framework: Intention in 4 steps

The I-AM model (detailed in Chapter 1) provided an explanation of how intention works. The next few pages describe a new tool— the IDEA framework—an effective, tried and tested model that will help you harness the power of intention.

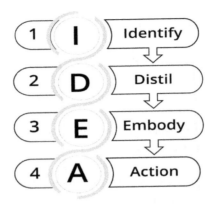

Figure 10: The IDEA Framework © 2019 Intentional Creations

The framework will help you to get started by identifying initial intentions; this is often the hardest part of the process. You then distil your intention by sense-checking it, testing it and, refining it if necessary. This is very important because intentions identified in Step 1 may be vague, slightly off at a tangent, or overly influenced by others' wants and desires.

Steps 3 and 4 set to work to deliver your intention by getting your grey matter working in the background. You start to embody your intention by walking the talk and grabbing opportunities that will help you towards the achievement of your intention.

The next four chapters detail the IDEA framework in far greater depth.

Things you need to know before getting started

Powerful intentions start with a deep, sincere desire (DSD), underpinned by a belief that it is possible. In order to identify your DSD and helpful/unhelpful beliefs, you need to engage both your mind and brain. Here are a couple of things that may sound counter-intuitive that you need to know before you get started.

Hold your intentions lightly

If you really want something with every fibre of your body, its easy to fall into the trap of over-striving. Striving to achieve desired goals can be a very positive thing, but over-striving can have the opposite effect. Although it may feel counter-intuitive, try to hold your intentions lightly. Be clear and concise about what your intention is, but don't get too caught up in the detail of how and when. This helps your brain to remain in an optimum state to notice each and every opportunity arising to transform your intentions into realities. Let your intentions manifest themselves naturally; they may do so in unexpected ways.

Listen to both your logic and your gut instinct

When making a decision, top leaders gather all the facts, study all the data, make a provisional decision then tune into their gut instinct. If it does not 'feel' right, they don't do it.

In Chapter 2, I outlined the wisdom of the 100 million neuronal connections in your gut. Your gut can help you tune into your unconscious responses, helping you to work more effectively with intentions. If you have a gut instinct something isn't quite right, trust it. It's not just your gut that can give you an insight into your inner wisdom; your whole body can. Your body often responds with physical tension to certain thoughts. This physical tension may indicate something isn't quite right, enabling you to check and refine your intentions. If you are not that body aware, mindfulness training can help. Discover more about this in Chapter 10.

Do your beliefs support or undermine you?

For an intention to become a reality, your deep, sincere desire for something to happen must be underpinned by a belief that it is possible. Whilst you may really want something to happen, you might not fully believe that it is possible. Any unconscious lack of belief is likely to impede or stop your intention from happening. The last few pages of this chapter provide valuable information on belief, to stop your beliefs from derailing your intentions.

Beliefs are conditioned perceptions built as a result of your interpretation of—and emotional responses to—good and bad experiences.

Your belief systems are psychological rules of command that your mind sends to your brain's nervous system. These rules shape your thoughts and form a filter or lens through which you experience reality. Over a lifetime, your beliefs become hard-wired into your brain and are reinforced every time you think in that way. These commands influence how you observe, distort, generalise or delete life's experiences.

In essence, beliefs are assumptions you make about yourself and others, shaping your expectations of the world and creating powerful stories of how things will be. Everyone uses beliefs as anchors to help them make sense of the world.

Your beliefs form the foundations of your expectations in life. All Humans crave certainty, because it creates a sense of safety and security, thereby reducing stress, anxiety and fear. Beliefs help you create a sense of certainty and security, explaining why you often hold onto them when they are irrelevant or no longer serve you well.

It's easy to fall into the trap of mistaking beliefs for facts. Beliefs are nothing more than assumptions or conclusions based on your experiences. Beliefs formed in childhood may no longer be relevant to your life as an adult and may prove unhelpful or even damaging.

Your beliefs can become tangled up with your language patterns, influencing your perception of life events and diverting you away from present-moment facts.

Perception + attention = experience

Every moment of your life, your five senses are collecting information that helps you to shape your perception of the world. Although the eyes are capable of receiving over one megabyte of information a second, most people can only consciously process four to five pieces at a time. Attention is a scarce and precious resource.

Your experience of the world is therefore determined by your perception (data gathered through the senses), and the things you choose to pay attention to.

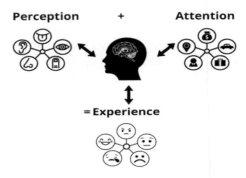

Figure 11: Perception + attention = experience © 2019 Intentional Creations

Harvard researchers Killingsworth and Gilbert researched the amount of time that the mind wandered[1]. Their conclusion was that your attention is not where you want it to be for almost 50% of the day. If this is the case, 50% of the day you are not consciously in control of the things you pay attention to. This may help to explain how easy it can be to build and strengthen your beliefs in the face of overwhelming present moment facts which (if you paid attention to them) would contradict or overturn your beliefs. In the early stages of a belief, your mindset remains flexible. Over time, as your brain actively seeks to collect more information to support each belief, the beliefs become stronger and more robust.

Beliefs become unconsciously reinforced and hard-wired into your brain via neuroplasticity. The more you think a certain way, the more likely you are to default to thinking in that way.

Eventually, your belief is so deeply ingrained and difficult to change.

Strong beliefs can be formed even when there is little or no real-world evidence to support them. You have faith because you desperately want to believe something. When you desperately want to believe something, it's easy to ignore the facts and use your imagination to help you gather together the things required to support that belief. This can be further reinforced by spending time with people who share your faith, who help you establish a firm belief—based on opinion and not fact.

When working with intention, try to be aware of any beliefs that may inhibit your progress, and gently test their validity and helpfulness.

Intention case studies

In the preparation of this book, I documented five case studies to illustrate the very different pathways people follow to turn their intentions into real-world events. I have featured Helen's case study in Chapters 6-9. To make this book accessible, I decided to publish it in this handy pocket book format. The downside of this is that I have insufficient space to share all five case studies in the book. You will find the following case studies on my website: www.intention-matters.com.

Case study 2: Advik

Advik is an Indian social entrepreneur, who owns a company that builds solar-powered portable water purification equipment for the developing world. His starting point for working with intention was his desire to make clean water accessible for all in India. Advik's case study illustrates one way to work with a mega intention.

Case study 3: Fernando

Fernando is a young, energetic, ideological Brazilian technical entrepreneur. He works part-time earning an income as a virtual reality programmer. The remainder of his time is devoted to the start-up of a social tech venture that seeks to 'wake up the world by using immersive technology in a positive way'. Fernando's case study illustrates another way to work with a mega intention.

Case study 4: Natasha

Natasha climbed the career ladder, gaining a senior role in a well-known marketing company. In her late 30's, she decided to give up work to become a full-time mum. After a period of time enjoying being a full-time parent, she felt the urge to work again. This was Natasha's starting point for working with intention. Natasha's case study illustrates one way to work with a core intention.

Case study 5: Hank

Hank is a singular individual who has a wealth of practical skills and is great at problem-solving. He's a skilled carpenter, and can turn his hands to most building projects. He lives 'off grid' on a small piece of land he owns, tucked away out of sight. Over the years, he has built a small house and outbuildings with free recycled materials. He collects rainwater and generates some of his own electricity, supplementing his power needs with a 1950s generator. Hank earns a subsistence income doing DIY and building work for people he likes, who are happy to put up with his idiosyncratic ways in order to get quality workmanship. His intention is to be as self-sufficient as possible. Hank's case study illustrates ways of working with core and micro intentions.

Summary

- ✎ The IDEA helps you work with intentions by:
    1. Identifying initial intentions
    2. Distilling, testing and refining your intention
    3. Embodying and embedding intention
    4. Taking action by noticing and grabbing opportunities that will help you towards the achievement of your intention.

- ✎ Maintain an optimum brain state and avoid over-striving by holding your intentions lightly.

- ✎ Listen to your gut instinct and body wisdom instead of relying solely on left brain logic.

- ✎ Remember that perception + attention = experience. When working with intention, try to be aware of any beliefs that may inhibit your progress, and gently test their validity and helpfulness.

- ✎ Some people find rituals help them to work with intentions. Rituals are not essential, but if you find them useful, create your own and use it to help you embody your intentions.

- ✎ There are many different ways of working with the

IDEA model. To illustrate this, Helen's case study is shared with you in Chapters 6-9. You can access more case studies from my website below.

🙌 Additional resources and case studies that support this chapter are available from my website: www. intention-matters.com

References

1. Killingsworth MA., Gilbert DT. (2010). *A wandering mind is an unhappy mind.* Science. 2010 Nov 12;330(6006):932. doi: 10.1126/science.1192439.

2. Damisch L, Stoberock B, Mussweiler T. (2010). *Keep your fingers crossed!: how superstition improves performance.* Psychological science Jul;21(7):1014-20. doi: 10.1177/0956797610372631. Epub 2010 May 28.

3. Nobel, Carmen. (2013). The Power of Rituals in Life, Death, and Business – Harvard Business School working paper (2013) Harvard Business School working paper 3rd June 2013.

4. Norton, Michael I., and Francesca Gino. (2013) *Rituals Alleviate Grieving for Loved Ones, Lovers, and Lotteries.* Journal of experimental psychology.

Chapter 6

Step 1: Identifying your intentions

"Intention is one of the most powerful forces there is. What you mean when you do a thing will always determine the outcome. The law creates the world."

– Brenna Yovanoff, bestselling author

In this chapter:

- ❧ *What's your deep, sincere desire?*
- ❧ *Identifying what you want*
- ❧ *Why rationality may be an illusion*
- ❧ *Tools and techniques to identify your intentions*
- ❧ *Step one case study*

This chapter has been written with the intention to help you to apply Step 1 of the IDEA framework—'Initiate' to identify as a starting point for your work with intention. Step 1 is sometimes the toughest part of the process. Take your time, allow yourself to take some wrong turns in order for you to find a way forward that really works for you.

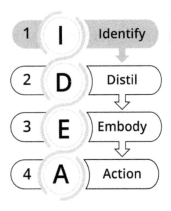

Figure 12: Step 1 of the IDEA framework © 2019 Intentional Creations

My father, a wise man, once told me "you can't guide a stationary vehicle". Perplexed, I asked him to explain. He told me that in life, it's important to keep moving. It does not matter if you end up going in the wrong direction for a while, as doing so helps you to work out the right way to go. If you stand still, nothing happens; you are simply stationary. When you move, things happen and opportunities arise. If you make a mistake, the people around you, your environment, and your inner compass will eventually help you navigate in the right direction.

Making a start is often the hardest part of initiating your intention. There is no time like the present; in fact, it's the only moment you have.

Remember that the next step of the process is Distilling, so you will have plenty of time to sense-check, test, and refine. This stage of the IDEA process is purely about getting started with your journey, so let go of the pressure to be perfect or get it right first time. There is plenty of time.

Putting yourself under unnecessary pressure to perform simply makes the process harder, or more time-consuming—so be kind to yourself and allow yourself as much time as you need.

What's your deep, sincere desire?

Powerful intentions start with a 'Deep, Sincere Desire' (DSD). If you want your intentions to turn into real-world events, they must start with something you really want at a very deep level.

Do you know what you want?

What do you want? What question could be more simple—or important—to answer? From publishing a bestselling book, to travelling the world, to taking a step forward, the story of your life is driven by your desires. But as easy as the question may be, answering it is often anything but.

"I don't know what I want, but I want it now"!

In Vivian Stanshall's wonderfully idiosyncratic film, 'Sir Henry at Rawlinsons End' (1980), Sir Henry, the matriarch of the stately pile known as 'Rawlinsons End', awakes early one morning and bellows at his servant "I don't know what I want, but I want it now"! Many people spend the majority of their lives not knowing what they want, or why they want it. Knowing how a Deep, Sincere, Desire (DSD) feels is a good starting point.

How does a DSD feel?

When working with nested, core, and mega intentions, your DSD is your strongest wish. It's the thing that literally makes your heart sing. It's the thing you would do if there were no payment involved, you love it that much. You might even pay someone to let you do it; that's how much you love this thing. Have you heard the expression "Follow your heart"? This is what I am talking about.

Your DSD is something that when you do it, or even just think about it, you get a warm feeling inside, particularly in the chest region. You may even feel a warm tingle over your whole body. It may trigger thoughts, images, and positive emotions. Superficial passing desires or goals simply do not have the same impact on your mind and brain.

A DSD coupled with belief that the thing you really want is achievable is the starting point of setting intentions that could change your life. At this point, knowing exactly how you will make your wish into reality does not matter, and must not restrict your thinking. The important thing is that you really want it with every fibre or your body, and believe it is possible. More about this in the next chapter.

Knowing the difference between DSDs and superficial wants

The culture in which you live may make you think you need things that in reality you don't, can't afford or that don't make you happy. You may have also become sucked into a herd mentality, wanting what others want or what others tell you is necessary for happiness.

Modern-day life can make it hard to differentiate between something you really want and a passing fancy or something that society or consumerism dictates you should aspire to. What if you only had six months to live; what would you do differently? What would be important to you?

Remember, your DSD is your strongest wish. It's the thing that literally makes your heart sing, palpable in every fibre of your body. Dropping the things that are not important requires you to connect to the DSD. The whole way that the intention system works is that it quickly alerts you to what NOT to do, provided the intention has been set. Mindfulness training really can help you in this process (more on this in Chapter 10).

Things to remember in Step 1

Here are some things that may sound counter-intuitive, that you need to know before you get started.

Left isn't always best

Our modern life and educational system have promoted a highly left-hemisphere-friendly way of doing and learning.

The most effective way to work with intention is to embrace your "messy" right hemisphere. This will enable you to move beyond pure reason and logic and tune into deeper, subtler signals. Connecting to subtle signals in the body and the heart may require some practice and effort at first, especially if you do not practice mindfulness, but your efforts will be richly rewarded. Your left-brain bias may result in a strong desire to use logic and "think about" rather than "feel into" decisions. This is perfectly normal, but be aware that other options may contribute to greater success.

Rationality may be an illusion

Your conscious mind controls a minute percentage of all your brain activities, so you are not as in control of your decisions as you might think. Neither are you as rational as you might think. Research by Bechara and Damasio[1] on the illusion of rationality clearly illustrates this, showing how the conscious and unconscious mind often crafts elaborate stories about why we do things, and why we feel the way we do—which may be partially or completely untrue.

We often invest so much in the story of who we are and what we do, that we fail to recognise the truth.

When working with intention, it's wise to playfully question both the things you aspire to achieve and your beliefs. Don't let rationality or logic get in the way of initiating intention. Ideas that may seem crazy or irrational are often the start of something amazing or a paradigm shift. Steps 2 and 3 will prompt you to sense-check and refine your initial intention later, if necessary.

The fearful brain

As detailed in Chapter 2, the human brain has evolved to be hyper-vigilant of any potential risks or threats, leading to what psychologists call 'the human negativity bias'. This, coupled with rapid change, technological advances, information overload and the fast pace of life can result in a long-term fearful, threat mode of brain operation. This has huge impacts on productivity, relationships at work, and well-being. When working with organisations, I frequently notice that management and leadership decision-making is driven by a lack of trust, fear, the need to protect oneself, and assumptions.

In this mode, it's very difficult to be truly creative, flexible, confident, innovative, and kind. When initiating an intention, watch out for your inbuilt negativity bias. Ask yourself 'If I had no fear and no barriers, what would my true intention be?' Alternatively, when you have identified an initial intention, ask yourself 'would this be the same or different if I had no barriers and no fear?'

Step 1 case study

We have used Helen's Case study in Chapters 6 to 9 to illustrate each of the four stages of the IDEA framework.

Helen is a hardworking, driven, highly motivated senior manager working for a FTSE 100 global insurance specialist. I met up with Helen for a coaching session, when I asked her what her intentions were. Helen listed a number of work-related goals:

- ❧ To enhance her communication skills.

- To become better at motivating her team.

- To support and manage change better.

- To improve staff retention within her division.

I questioned why she really wanted to achieve these? She looked at me in disbelief and told me with some force that these were perfectly logical goals and things she intended to achieve. I smiled inwardly and re-phrased the question, asking "why are these important to you?" Helen paused, then after some thought replied:

- I want to make my company, and especially my division a really great place to work

- I want to support, empower, and develop my staff

- I want to be recognised as a great leader, gaining promotion, and access to new and exciting challenges at work.

So Helen's starting point for initiating intention was her work-related goals. After further consideration, she refined these into three work-related initial intentions. Next, I helped Helen to test her belief in her ability to make this happen. Helen had a strong belief in her ability to achieve these intentions, and a strong desire to make them happen. Helen originally thought these were her core intentions, but as you will discover in the next chapter when working through Step 2, this changed.

Techniques to help you identify intentions

Your starting point for initiating intention may be very different from Helen's. Start this step wherever feels right for you or with whatever comes to mind.

The aim of Step 1 of the IDEA framework is to initiate intention, to make a start by identifying one or more intention(s) and test your belief that it or they will happen. Some people, like Helen, find it easiest to start with goals and then identify initial intentions later leading to the identification of core intention. Others such as Advik, Natasha and Fernando, featured in our case studies, have a very different starting point.

Advik started with what he thought was his core intention and later discover his true intention, which turned out to be much bigger. Natasha identified a broad core intention but initially lacked belief in it happening, as she didn't know where to start. Fernando was strongly motivated to make a difference in the world.

Whilst he had a strong belief he could make things happen, his mega intention was so big, he lacked the experience to know where to start. One size does not fit all; we are all individuals, so experiment and see what works best for you. Pick one or more of the following tools to help you initiate your intention—or find another method that works for you

Initiating intention tool one: Get moving!

Making a start is often the hardest part of initiating your intention. There is no time like the present; in fact, it's the only moment you have. Grab a pen and paper, or a tablet. Starting with whatever comes to mind, try to identify:

1. What is your core intention?

2. Do any nested intentions (or interim intentions) sit below this?

3. What realistic broad goals can you set yourself to get you moving?

If you feel resistant or sense a block, a little mindfulness (see Chapter 10) can be beneficial. Focus your attention on your present-moment experience. Pay attention to the process, not just the outcomes. Notice:

- How did you approach this task?

    - Did you procrastinate or jump up and find a pen?

    - What can your approach to this task tell you about the more subconscious data feeding into this project idea?

- How did you place the pen on the paper (or finger to tablet)?

    - The pressure?

    - The speed of writing?

Do not get too bogged down when working through Step 1. Identifying just one intention is a great place to start. It does not matter if it's a core intention, a nested intention or simply a goal. It's a starting point. Step 2 will help you distil, test and refine it as necessary.

Initiating intention tool two: Mind mapping

Mind mapping is a great way of getting information in and out of your brain. Mind mapping is both a creative and logical way of making notes that visually "maps out" your ideas. Mind maps have a natural structure radiating from the centre and using lines, symbols, words, colour and images that are brain-friendly.

If you are new to mind mapping, bring to mind a map of a city. The city centre represents the main idea; the main roads leading from the centre represent the key thoughts or considerations. Secondary roads or branches represent your secondary thoughts, and so on. Special images or shapes can represent landmarks of interest or particularly relevant ideas.

Mind mapping helps you to jot ideas down in any order, as they arise in your head. You are not restrained by having to think in a linear fashion. It allows you to note down any and all ideas, knowing you can reorganise them later. Mind mapping can be via pen and paper—there are neurological benefits in using pen and paper—or via the many mind-mapping software products available.

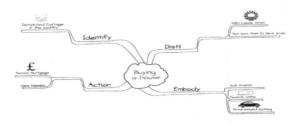

Figure 13: Creating a mind map. © 2019 Intentional Creations

Initiating intention tool three: Gaining a felt sense of your intention

Bring to mind your intention. Tune into it as vividly as possible, just as if it were happening at this moment. Engage as many senses as possible.

- What does it look like?
- What is your emotional state?

  Are any negative, positive or neutral emotions present?

- What can you hear? Smell?
- How does it feel?

  Does it feel right or can you detect any uneasiness?

  Has any tension arisen in the body?

- Are you moving all or part of your body? How is your body moving?

If you experience any uneasiness or negative emotions, or detect tension arising in the body, this may be a sign that your intention isn't resonating with you at a subconscious or gut level. Use the mind-mapping tool (See tool 6 above) or sense-checking tools above to help you make sense of what's going on, and to pinpoint what needs refining.

Initiating Intention tool four: Coaching

Coaches help you identify and focus on what's important, accelerating your success. An intention coach can help you to:

- ❧ Create a safe environment in which you see yourself more clearly.

- ❧ Identify the difference between goals and intentions.

- ❧ Lead you towards more intentional thought, actions and behaviours.

You will find more tools and techniques on my website below.

Summary

When *identifying* your intentions:

- ❧ Getting started can be the hardest part. Sometimes, it's better to do *something,* even if it turns out later not to be the right thing. Mistakes, detours, and wrong turns point you in the right directions.

- ❧ Check how much you want your intention. If it's superficial or someone else's dream, let it go.

- ❧ When identifying your intention, use all the resources available to you. Use your left-brain logic, right-brain creativity, body wisdom and gut instinct.

- Don't let fear be a barrier. Acknowledge and accept your fear if it arises. Don't let it hijack you or push you off course.

- Additional resources and case studies that support this chapter are available from my website: www. intention-matters.com

References

1. Bechara A., Damasio AR, Damasio H, Anderson SW. (1994). *Insensitivity to future consequences following damage to human prefrontal cortex.* Cognition. 1994 Apr-Jun;50(1-3)

Chapter 7

Step 2: Distilling and refining your intention

"Ask yourself: What is my truest intention?
Give yourself time to let a 'yes' resound
within you. When it's right, I guarantee that
your entire body will feel it."

– Oprah Winfrey, talk show host, actress,
producer

In this chapter:

- ❧ *How to distil and refine your intentions*

    - ❧ *Checking your bias*

    - ❧ *Being both specific and flexible*

    - ❧ *Checking in with your beliefs*

- ❧ *Step 2 case study*

- ❧ *Tools and techniques to help you distil your*
  intention

Congratulations! You have reached Step 2 of the IDEA framework. Step 1 is often the hardest part of the process. Step 2 builds on Step 1 by helping you to sense-check your intention, distilling it, testing it, and refining it as necessary.

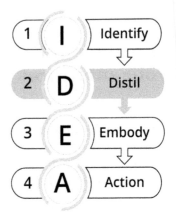

Figure 14: Step 2 of the IDEA framework © 2019 Intentional Creations

At this stage, it's easy to zoom off on a wave of excitement, heading as fast as you can to the stage where things start to happen and your intention becomes a real-world event. Sometimes, you need to slow down in order to speed up!

Setting off on your journey with a loose, ill-defined intention in which you lack belief or that may not be what you really want, will only waste time and may lead to disappointment, a lack of results, or an immature manifestation of an intention.

Intention drives attention to deliver actions that make things happen in the real world

Intentions come in all shapes and sizes

Intentions and the scale of intentions vary from person to person. There is no right or wrong intention. If your intentions are modest and self-contained, there's no need to reach further or aspire towards mega intentions. You should work with the intention(s) that feel right for you at this moment.

As detailed in Chapter 1, Figure 3, I have split intentions into four categories:

- ❧ **Mega intentions** – huge, potentially world-changing intentions. Mega intentions are not for the faint-hearted and may take a lifetime to achieve or even get started. If you surface a mega intention in Step One of the process, you will definitely need to break it down into core and nested intentions. Failure to do this may lead to overwhelm, procrastination, fear and not getting started at all. Advik and Fernando's case studies from Chapter 5 are examples of this.

- ❧ **Core intentions** – Life-changing intentions. Smaller in scale and more self contained than mega intentions. May contribute to the achievement of mega intentions or stand alone. Natasha and Hank's case studies from Chapter 5 are examples of this

- ❧ **Nested intentions** - Intentions that, when achieved, contribute to the achievement of your core intention. You might initially identify these as core intentions, then later discover a greater or more overarching intention to which this intention contributes. Helen's case studies from the previous chapter turned out to be nested intentions, as you will discover later in this chapter.

🐍 **Micro intentions** – Day or instant, moment-changing intentions, small in scale but with a potentially big impact.

Things to remember in Step 2

When working with intent, and especially at the 'refining it' stage, it's important to not give in to self-limiting beliefs, doubts, or the voice of your inner bully.

Check your bias

Your conscious mind controls a minute percentage of all your brain activities, so you are not as in control of your decisions as you might think. Neither are you as rational as you might think. Research by Bechara and Damasio on the illusion of rationality clearly illustrates this.

Your conscious and unconscious mind often crafts elaborate stories about why you do things, and why you feel the way you do—which may be partially or completely untrue.

You often invest so much in the story of who you are and what you do, that you fail to recognise the truth. That uncomfortable truth is that you often want things and therefore do things that can make you base, selfish, self-righteous, and unjust—and this applies to all of us.

It's valuable to pause and ask yourself what exactly you want. It is vital to separate this from what you think you should want or what others *want you to want*, or want for you. For example, I want this book to become a bestseller; I want it to help my readers harness the power of intent and have a positive impact on their lives.

I want writing a book to be easier. I want people to be kinder and more considerate to one another. I want politicians to be honest.... and the list goes on.....! It's worth spending some time to explore your wants and desires in order to help you to focus on what your true intent is.

Be specific but flexible

A potentially tricky part of Step 2 of the IDEA process is trying to be as specific as possible; even harder is doing this without shutting down or inhibiting the possibilities and opportunities arising in Steps 3 and 4 of the process.

If you are not specific enough about your intentions, you may end up with an immature manifestation of an intention. When you fail to adequately specify what you truly want, you may get exactly what you asked for—but find it isn't what you actually need.

For example, setting an intention to have a boyfriend like Johnny Depp might deliver you a boyfriend that looks like Johnny but has terrible social skills, low intellect and flies into a temper at the slightest provocation. The trick is to be specific but hold your intention lightly. Perfecting this can take time and patience. There's a lot that can be learnt from failures. Sir

James Dyson famously built 5,127 prototypes and spent more than 15 years to develop this iconic vacuum cleaner. Thankfully, in my experience, most people achieve, or at least start to achieve their intentions in far less time than this!

Do your beliefs support or undermine your intentions?

As mentioned previously, your belief systems are psychological rules of command that your mind sends to your brain's nervous system. These rules shape your thoughts and form a filter or lens through which you experience reality. Beliefs are assumptions that you make about yourself and about others; they shape your expectations of the world around you and create powerful stories of how things will be.

Your beliefs influence every aspect of your life, every moment of the day. Beliefs:

- Shape your expectations and perceptions of reality.

- Influence the decisions you make and your choices in life.

- Determine the questions you ask yourself throughout the day, influencing your ability to think creatively, constructively, and critically.

- Determine how you feel about yourself, how you feel about others, and how you feel about the events and circumstances of your life.

- Determine the things you will or won't do.

🦢 Shape the targets you set yourself, how you work to accomplish them, and your ability to assess your progress towards achieving those goals.

Beliefs have three distinct parts:

Psychological Rules: the rules that support your beliefs, often stemming from pain or pleasure. In other words, your perception and interpretation of what gives you pain and pleasure affects the end outcome.

Global Beliefs: generalised beliefs you make about things, about people, and about life. Global beliefs are things you don't give much thought to, accepting them as being the truth without question. For example "I am...", "Life is...", "People are..."

Convictions - Beliefs that have the highest unwavering certainty, commitment, and dedication. These strong beliefs are often immune to logic. Often built up over a long time based on emotion, time, energy, and thought, they can be difficult to change. Many deep-seated convictions you have about life may be held at an unconscious level, leading to 'autopilot' habitual patterns that make it difficult to imagine other alternative possibilities.

When distilling your intention, try to develop an awareness of your psychological rules, beliefs and convictions. This awareness will help you override unhelpful beliefs that may only serve to get in your own way.

Using mindfulness to distil and refine intention

Mindfulness is the art of paying attention to what's going on moment by moment, assessing this information in a way that is calm and focussed. It is a great asset when refining your intention.

For more about mindfulness, see Chapter 10. It allows you to tap into feedback from your body and emotions, providing multi-dimensional ways to sense-check decisions, ideas and intentions.

If unfamiliar with mindfulness, you may be tempted to try to apply logic to determine if your intention(s) is/are right for you at this moment. Although this may seem a rational thing to do, it may not be helpful.

Many think brain processing is a top-down activity. Recent research is making it apparent just how much information is passed to the brain 'bottom up' via the vagus nerve. The gut, sometimes referred to by scientists as 'the little brain', hosts a massive number of nerves different to those in the rest of the body. The little brain is as large and chemically complex as the grey matter in the brain; the gut is therefore responsible for how you feel, guiding your emotional state. It sends messages to the insula, limbic system, prefrontal cortex, amygdala and hippocampus, thus helping govern your self-awareness, emotions, moral compass, fears, memories and motivations.

Mindfulness training helps you to tune into some of the messages sent bottom-up from your gut to your brain, helping you to tap into your inner wisdom, providing fresh insights and new perspectives. In the tool section of this chapter, you will find two mindfulness-based exercises to help you work with Step 2.

Step 2 case study

After identifying some initial intentions in a coaching session, Helen (whom you met in Chapter 6) was tasked with spending some time to consider her core intent for her life and career; what was important, and what she really wanted in life if there were no constraints?

Several weeks later, we met up again. Helen said that she had found this a valuable exercise. When she stripped away the layers, what she really wanted—her core intentions—were to:

- ❧ Become the best leader it was possible to be.
- ❧ Earn a sufficient income to live comfortably in her house, and do the things in life she loved to do.

Helen had a strong belief in her ability to achieve her core intention, a belief that I shared. So, for Helen, the easiest way to identify her core intention was to start with goals, then identify her nested intentions, helping her to identify her core intention.

Helen was very clear that her core intention was to earn a sufficient income to live comfortably in her house and do the things in life she loved to do. It felt right at every level and I was pleased to hear she had reached this conclusion.

Despite this, she was initially filled with self-doubt and fear that she could ever achieve her core intention to earn a sufficient income to live comfortably in her house and do the things in life she loved to do. Her parents had always struggled to make ends meet when she was a child; this had motivated her to work hard in her career, so she would never live her life in the same position of fear and impoverishment as her parents.

It was only when working to refine and embed her intention, that she realised that she still had a deep-seated fear of poverty, that she wouldn't have quite enough money, and that life would always be a struggle for her. By surfacing these fears and her mental wiring about money, she was able to work to hardwire in new, more positive and open-minded attitudes towards money.

The aim of Step 2 of the Intention Formula is to distil, test and refine the intention(s) you identified in Step 1. Some people, like Helen, radically change their intentions as part of Step 2. Others like Advik expand and broaden their intention. Maybe like Natasha and Fernando, you need to explore what your intention looks like, and indeed return to this stage several times as you move forward, discovering what works for you, what you want, and—importantly—what you don't want. Maybe like Hank, the intent you identified in Step 1 remains steadfast and true?

The point is, there is no 'one size fits all' way to work with this model. The four-step IDEA formula simply provides a framework for working effectively with intention.

Techniques to help you distil your intention

Your starting point for distilling your intention may be very different from Helen's. Start this step wherever feels right for you or with whatever comes to mind.

As with stage one, there is no one 'right' or 'wrong' place to start, and I again encourage you to experiment and see what works best for you. Whilst it would be useful for you to clearly identify both your core and nested intentions, don't worry if this does not happen or you can't decide if an intention is core and nested. In this instance, just pick an intention and make a start.

Pick one or more of the following tools to help you distil your intention. I recommend that you ideally use two tools to help you to consolidate, confirm, or refine your intention. You will find more techniques on my website.

Distilling intention tool one: Pick the low-hanging fruit

1. Bring to mind your intention. If it's a mega intention, try to break it down to a number of core or nested intentions. Write them down on a piece of paper if you feel it helps.

2. Consider the possible opportunities already available or open to you. Which ones are the 'low hanging fruit'—the opportunities already within your grasp and easier to pick?

3. Although you may feel compelled to pick all the fruit all at once, why not start by simply focussing on the opportunities already within your reach? Avoid procrastination and overwhelm by making these your starting point.

Distilling intention tool two: De-chunking a mega intention

How do you eat an elephant? (or a chocolate cake the size of a mountain?!) The answer? One teaspoon at a time. If you are driven towards a huge mega intention and have a strong belief it's possible, it's still necessary to break the intention into a number of smaller ones and work towards the achievement of the whole, one small teaspoon at a time. This technique might be a good way to get you started.

1. Write your mega intention at the top of a sheet of paper.

2. Write on scraps of paper or Post-It notes the intentions that could contribute to the achievement of the mega intention. Try not to get bogged down in the small details, remaining as 'big picture' as possible.

3. Now take time to consider the things you have written on the papers. Ask yourself if these are:

    a) Mega intentions that supersede or replace the mega intention you started with?

    b) Core intentions (substantial intentions that contribute to the achievement of the mega intention)?

    c) Nested intentions (intentions that contribute to the achievement of the core intention)?

    d) Goals or other things that contribute to the achievement of a nested intention?

4. Rearrange the pieces of paper until you identify two or more core intentions, positioning other notes below that, to represent nested intentions.

Note: If you are unclear of the differences between core intentions, nested intentions and goals, refer back to Chapter 1 or look to the Glossary for more information.

Distilling intention tool three: Whose voice is it?

Ask yourself if your intention is actually yours, or is it someone else's? It's an easy mistake to make.

My mother trained as a doctor but did not complete the last part of her training, and bitterly regretted it. When I decided on which exams to work towards at secondary school, my choices were based on the idea that I was going to train to be a doctor. Only after completing my exams did I realise I had no interest whatsoever in becoming a doctor and pursued a completely different career path. This tool will help you check if your intention is truly yours or someone else's.

1. Use your logical brain first. Ask yourself if your intention is what you really want. Note down the logical answers you receive.

2. Check in with your body. Bring to mind your intention. How does it feel in your body? What emotions are triggered? Make a note.

3. Now bring to mind three people who are influential in your life. They might include parents, best friends, work colleagues, a wise leader, a teacher or university lecturer.

   a. Would your influential friends approve or aspire towards your intention?

b. It does not really matter either way, just check in and see what arises within you, with an open and curious mind.

4. Ask yourself if the intention is truly, uniquely and individually yours? Is it your intention, or someone else's?

Distilling intention tool four: Mindfully sitting with your intention

If you are experienced with mindfulness, you should be able to guide yourself through this exercise. If you are less experienced, you might like to download my free MP3 exercise IM1 guide you through.

- Select the intention you wish to distil or refine.

- Settle yourself into a comfortable upright chair with both feet connected to the ground and your arms resting comfortably on your lap.

- Sit in a chair in an upright, open and confident posture, with the shoulders relaxed and not slumped backwards or leaning forwards. Alert but relaxed.

- Spend a few minutes focusing your full attention on the present-moment sensations of breathing. Use the physical sensations of the breath coming in and breath going out as an anchor to steady your attention.

- Bring to mind the intention you have identified.

- What sensations are present in the body? Where? Try to be as specific as possible.

∾ Visualising it happening. Watch it like a movie, looking at the still images that may arise, or getting a 'felt sense' of your intention becoming a reality. What arises in body, heart, images, thoughts? Where does the mind want to flow?

∾ If it feels right for you, place your hand on your heart, connecting with what's true for you. How does the heart feel about this intention?

∾ Let go of your intention now. Return your attention to your breath and once more spend a few minutes focussing your attention on the present-moment sensations of breathing, feeling the breath coming in, and the breath going out.

∾ Finish by widening your attention to notice how your whole body feels as you sit in your chair in your room, in this unique moment.

∾ When ready to do so, open your eyes, ready for the rest of the day ahead.

∾ Journal if you wish.

Summary

When distilling your intentions, remember:

∾ Intentions come in all shapes and sizes. Pick an intention that is right for you at this moment. Big isn't always best!

∾ Be aware of any unhelpful bias you may possess.

∾ Try to be specific but remain open and flexible.

∾ Check if your beliefs support or undermine your intentions.

- Consider using mindfulness to help you refine your intentions.

- If you don't know where to start or are experiencing procrastination, pick the low-hanging fruit.

- Additional resources and case studies that support this chapter are available from my website: www. intention-matters.com

Chapter 8

Step 3: Embodying your intentions

" The more aware of your intentions and your experiences you become, the more you will be able to connect the two, and the more you will be able to create the experiences of your life consciously. This is the development of mastery. It is the creation of authentic power."

– Gary Zukav, author of four consecutive New York Times Bestsellers.

In this chapter:

- *How to embody and embed your intentions*

    - *Activating your will*

    - *Focussing your attention*

    - *Noticing your habits*

- *Step 3 Case study*

- *Tools and techniques to help you embody your intention*

In Step 1, you identified your initial intentions. In Step 2, you tested, sense-checked and refined your intentions. Step 3 of the IDEA framework will now help you to embody and *embed* your intention.

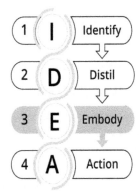

Figure 15: Step 3 of the IDEA framework. © 2019 Intentional Creations

Why embody? When I created this model, I initially called this step 'embed' – but I quickly realised this wasn't an adequate description of the stage. When you embody something, you make it a part of who you are, how you see your life, and how you live it. You absorb it, assimilate it, incorporate and integrate it into your life. It becomes blended and combined with your life. You and it merge and mingle. You start to represent your intention in visible form. This chapter will show you how to do this.

Things to remember in Step 3

In Steps 1 and 2, I suggested that you held your intention lightly. Intentions are very different from the carefully-planned and orchestrated SMART objectives you might find on a performance appraisal. Remember, intentions need to be held lightly, allowing them to embed and unfold in unexpected ways, taking action when opportunities arise, as you will discover later in this chapter.

Step 2 required you to check in with yourself and do a readiness check. If you have reached Step 3 and at some level are still not sure about your intentions, it may be a good idea to revisit Steps 1 and 2 again. Some people work through these steps two, three or even four times before they distil their intentions to perfection and they fully feel right. When your intention feels right—even if you haven't got the slightest clue how it will happen—do work through Step 3.

Activating your Will (AW)

What gets you out of bed in the morning? What activates your will when the alarm goes off and there may be a strong desire to stay in the warmth of your bed?

At the same time, you have a desire to get up and ready for work. The desire that is the stronger one wins and motivates you to take action, by either snuggling deeper into your duvet or stepping out of bed and into your shower.

Those who do step out of bed may do so not because they love their job, but because they are strongly motivated to earn money. To paraphrase the words of the Dalai Lama, many humans sacrifice their health in order to make money. Then they sacrifice money to recuperate their health. They are then so anxious about the future that they do not enjoy the present. As a result, they do not live in the present or the future; they live as if they are never going to die, and then they die having never really lived.

Money is needed to pay the mortgage, support families, take a holiday or acquire things to make your life easier or more pleasurable. But the pursuit of wealth is rarely a person's deep, sincere desire (DSD) and may inhibit the achievement of their true DSD.

Focussing your attention (FA)

Defining your DSD enables your mind to task your brain to focus its attention. Your brain then concentrates on ways of thinking and behaving that are likely to help you to achieve your DSD, often at a subconscious level.

Narrow focus vs. open monitoring

When your attention is narrowly focussed on a single thing, other internal and external stimuli are deliberately ignored. 'Open monitoring' allows attention to be focussed far more widely. When you set a DSD, it's important not to get tangled up in thoughts about exactly how you are going to make your wish a reality. Doing so will trip your brain into a narrow focus at a time when you need a much wider one—the ability to open monitor.

Open monitoring

When practising open monitoring, there is no specific focus of attention; instead, all salient internal and external stimuli are observed on a moment-by-moment basis as they arrive. Open monitoring is a broadening of attention, enabling you to be aware of all events and experiences arising in any given moment. You are essentially attempting to observe as much of your mental activity (including the sensing of the body) as possible, from as wide a view as you can.

Imagine a helicopter flying over the African plains and being able to see all sort of different animals, vegetation, and habitats. Learning to watch your mental activity in this way is a really effective way to break mental habits promptly.

A 2008 study[1] concluded that open monitoring decreased elaborative stimulus—the tendency to get caught up or sidetracked by one thing when the brain processes incoming information. This decrease enabled participants to improve the way their brain processed moment-to-moment stimuli. This made them less likely to get stuck or side-tracked on individual stimuli, and as a result, see the bigger picture.

Open monitoring cultivates metacognition, the ability to observe your thoughts, emotions and body-based responses. Open monitoring is useful when working with your DSD, providing sufficient perspective to see chains of mental events, and respond flexibly and kindly to distractions. It helps you to unravel old intentions and create new ones.

Becoming conscious of your subconscious

Your subconscious can sidetrack you and get in the way when you really need to focus your attention. Open monitoring enables you to become conscious of your subconscious.

Many people's modern-day experience of "racing thoughts" or having something they can't get out of their mind is a symptom of an overactive Default Mode Network (DMN).

Being aware of what is happening the background—activity in your DMN—as you go about your tasks and activities (doing mode) is a vital aspect of focussing your attention. Attention is re-harnessed and directed back to the present moment (or object or task) and then the default mode activation is reduced. Priority is given to the incoming sensory information, a vital aspect of attention, helping you to deliver your DSD.

Becoming aware of your habits

When you are trying to do something new or achieve something never achieved before, habits can get in the way.

Old habits that no longer serve you well are highly draining and can consume huge amounts of energy. Imagine if you could do a spring clean on this activity, teasing out what is helping you and what you can trim? Pruning creates space, making the whole system more efficient. You can!

Taking steps to identify some of your defaults (habits) that no longer serve you well can help your mind and brain to operate more efficiently.

Mindfulness can help you to cultivate the metacognition, the skill of open monitoring, becoming consciously aware of what you are thinking, seeing, and feeling in any given moment.

Research demonstrates that experienced meditators have a reduction in baseline DMN activity. It is thought this represents the "quietened" mind, one that is not overly active and agitated thinking about past or future, coupled with a strong attentional network muscle. It's important to stress that the meditation-based exercises forming a part of mindfulness are not designed to suppress DMN activity; rather, it's about noticing more and more promptly when the mind has wandered, and DMN activity has increased, and then choosing to reduce this activity by returning your focus to the present.

Embodying your intention

Once you have identified your intention, sense-checked it and refined it if required, the next step is embedding it into your brain and into your life so that you embody your intentions. At this stage it's important to be kind to yourself.

We are rarely taught to be kind to ourselves, to accept ourselves just as we are. The act of kindness and acceptance helps to switch down your sympathetic nervous system, (preparing you for danger), and switch up your parasympathetic nervous system, sometimes described as your 'rest and digest' system. This improves your mental clarity and ability to think creatively, helping you to both consciously and unconsciously work towards your goals.

Step 3 case study

In this section, I share with you Helen's case study to illustrate one way of initiating intention. Helen's way isn't the only way of working through Step 3 of the IDEA framework. See more case studies on my website.

Helen's core Intention was to become the best leader she could be and to earn a sufficient income to live comfortably in her house and do the things in life she loved to do.

Her nested intentions included the desire to be recognised as a great leader, and move onto greater challenges. Her goals were to improve communication, motivate her team, manage change better, and improve staff retention. It all seemed so clear and yet she felt stuck—and did not know what do next.

Helen decided to give her intentions a readiness check. She asked herself "What's important now?" and "Where do I want to put my energy"? She found herself thinking about her house, the kitchen she loved to cook in, her open-plan living spaces and outdoor terrace she loved to entertain on, as well as her friends visiting who lived nearby.

The answer became clear; she wanted to continue living there into old age. She had six years left to pay on the mortgage and decided she wanted to pay it off as soon as possible. Over the next few weeks, she reviewed her finances and increased her mortgage payments. She also set a new intention to apply for the Director's vacancy she had been dithering about. She reasoned that gaining this promotion would increase her earnings so she could pay off her mortgage two years earlier.

In addition, it would provide greater opportunities for her to develop her leadership capability. She imagined herself working as a Director, and found herself experiencing a sense of happiness, calm and competence. She pictured the day that her mortgage was fully paid off. She visualised her savings growing. She chuckled to herself as an image of a jaunty fat piggy bank overflowing with money appeared in her mind, trotting around her garden contentedly snuffling and grunting. She pictured the changes she would make in the company, with expansion and engaged, happy employees.

In Step 3, Helen checked in with the intentions she had set. She discovered what felt important for her at this moment. This spurred her to take actions, helping her to embody her intention. Her unusual visualisation helped her to embed and embody her intentions further.

Techniques to help you embed your intention

Pick one or more of the following tools to help you initiate your Intention, or find another method that works for you.

Embodiment tool one: Practical readiness check

In my case study, Helen conducted a practical readiness check. You may find this useful.

- Bring to mind your intention.

- Ask yourself 'what's important now?' Notice what arises. Make a note of what arises if it's helpful.

ཤ Ask yourself 'where can I best invest my energy now?'
Notice what arises. Make a note of what arises if it's
helpful.

Everything that arises will help you to crystallise your plans.
If, like Helen, you were planning to apply for a promotion,
and somehow when you ask the questions above it no longer
seems important— or if you feel resistance and it all seems like
too much effort,—again, go back to Step 2, or even Step 1.

If you ask 'what's important now?' and your intention feels right,
you will know you are on the right track. Asking 'where can I
best invest my energy?' may clarify a good starting point to
help you embody and embed your intention moving forwards.

Embodiment tool two: Journalling

The brain can only consciously juggle around four tasks
simultaneously. Your working memory is the bottleneck of your
brain. Writing down your intention on a sheet of paper does
a number of things. Firstly, it frees up your precious working
memory so you can focus on something else. Secondly, it helps
you to start to hard-wire it into your brain.

Writing it, or even drawing it into a journal or a specially-
selected book is better still, as it helps to emphasise to the brain
the importance you attach to it, making it easier to remember.

ཤ Make a note in your journal to capture your progress
and how this makes you feel.

ཤ Keep a note of :

o any themes that emerge.

- ○ any doubts that emerge.

- ○ any blockages that you encounter.

- ○ any things you over- or under-estimated.

- ○ Any wrong turns or feelings of failure.

- ○ Any immature manifestations of intentions (see below).

- ❧ Common themes that emerge may include procrastination or doubt before action, over-thinking, or certain behaviour patterns. Journaling will help you spot unhelpful patterns of thinking and behaviour. Once you notice these, you can decide when it's time to change the record. Wrong turns and failures are valuable learning experiences. Avoid wallowing in self-pity or blame. Learn from them and move forward.

Immature manifestations of intentions may arise. This means that you get exactly the thing you set an intention to gain, but when it arrives, it isn't what you want or need. It usually occurs when you are too vague when you set an intention, or you don't actually know what you want.

For example, you ask for a boyfriend like Johnny Depp and start dating a man that looks like Johnny Depp but in all other ways, he does not meet your needs. Your intention has become a reality but emerges in an immature state, so needs further time and growth to deliver what you really want and need.

Journalling, or simply regular reflection time, will help you to reinforce your sense of journey and progress, helping you to further embody your intent into your life.

Embodiment of intention tool three: visioning

In Step 2, you may have created a vision of how it feels to have matured your intention. If you have, do it again. If you haven't, give it a try; you can do this with or without the addition of a little mindfulness. Doing so (as detailed in Chapter 2) helps you to further embed it into your brain, and sets your brain to work at both a conscious and subconscious level to help you achieve your intent.

If you are an experienced meditator, you can guide yourself using the exercise below. Alternatively, you might wish to be guided through the exercise by listening to MP3 exercise IM2. Meditation is a powerful tool to help you to give instructions to your brain. However, if you'd rather not meditate, simply try building a stationary or moving picture in your mind's eye, and dwell for a short while in the vision you have created, engaging as many senses as possible.

If it feels right for you, you might wish to create a vision board, a collage of images, pictures and words that encapsulate your intentions. Vision boards can act as a source of inspiration and motivation to help you embody and embed your intentions.

From a brain perspective, vision boards or similar visual stimuli can prime your default mode network with visual images of what you want or desire. This brings a greater attentional focus to this (confirmation bias) and will also trigger you to notice more quickly when you are off-track and to do something about it. Creating a vision board is not a guarantee that your intentions will be delivered, but so long as you don't over-strive or obsess about it, and continue to hold your intentions lightly, they can trigger beneficial cognitive processes.

Visioning is strengthening the intention and belief in it, and this activates will. To do this activate your creative Right hemisphere by using symbols. If a picture worth a thousand words, a symbol is worth a thousand pictures. Find a picture or object that symbolises your intention. Place it somewhere you will see it regularly.

Embodiment of intention tool three: linking

Linking together information, ideas and experiences helps you to hard-wire your intention into your memory. Your brain accesses your stored memories via two main methods: recognition, and recall. Recognition is the association of an event (in this instance, setting an intention) with things you have previously experienced or encountered.

Recognition is largely unconscious. Recall involves remembering something that is not currently present—in this instance, retrieving a mental image or sense of the intent. The more you link your intention into the different aspects of your life, the more easily the brain can retrieve stored information about your intention. This helps you to speed up the process of manifesting your intention.

How does this intention play out in everyday actions and interactions?

What are the concrete indicators of this intention in your life?

What would this look like in a practical way, day to day?

Linking can be either conscious or unconscious. Examples of conscious linking might include:

- Linking your core intention to nested intentions and goals.

- Noticing when opportunities arise that might help you realise your intention.

- Linking helpful habitual behaviours and patterns of thinking to the achievement of your intention.

- Changing unhelpful habitual behaviours and patterns of thinking, and linking the new habits to the achievement of your intentions.

- Linking things happening in your life, with intentions.

Examples of unconscious linking might include:

- Linking a positive emotion, for example happiness or excitement, to your intention.

- Your unconscious brain remaining vigilant for activities and opportunities that might contribute towards the achievement of your intent.

Make an effort to seek positive ways to link anything and everything to your intention. The more links, the better.

Summary

When embedding and embodying intentions into your life:

- ❧ Various cognitive processes are triggered in your brain. These may include activating your will and focussing your attention via narrow or open monitoring.

- ❧ Remain vigilant and aware of the impact of your habits.

- ❧ Check and monitor your readiness.

- ❧ Additional resources and case studies that support this chapter are available from my website: www. intention-matters.com

References

1. Richard J. Davidson,RJ and Lutz, A. (2008). *Buddha's Brain: Neuroplasticity and Meditation*. IEEE Signal Process Mag. 2008 Jan 1; 25(1): 176–174.

Chapter 9

Step 4: Taking action

*"It is not good enough for things to be
planned – they still have to be done; for the
intention to become a reality, energy has to
be launched into operation."*

– Walt Kelly: political and philosophical
commentator.

In this chapter:

- ❧ *How intention makes things happen*

- ❧ *Knowing when to take action and when to let
  things be*

- ❧ *Maintaining momentum*

- ❧ *Step 4 case study*

- ❧ *Tools and techniques to help you take action to
  make your intention a reality.*

Step 4, the final stage of the IDEA framework, helps you to recognise when to take action and make things happen in the real world.

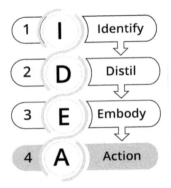

Figure 16: Step 4 of the IDEA framework. © 2019 Intentional Creations

Step 4 of the intention formula is about taking responsibility for your actions. This includes both knowing when it's time to take action, and knowing when to let things be and simply wait.

Taking action

Once you have set an intention and your mind and brain are working together to help you achieve it, it's time to take *action*—either passively or actively. As mentioned previously, be vigilant, looking out for opportunities that will help you towards your intention.

When taking action, it's important to monitor and manage

yourself to ensure you avoid putting yourself under excessive pressure; this will only stop you from achieving your intent. Turning an intention into reality can take time to emerge. Getting desperate or over-striving will activate the primitive brain's protection circuitry and reduce your ability to be creative, as well as to notice when opportunities arise that could help you achieve your goals.

Noticing and taking advantage of arising opportunities will lead to you taking action, as and when the time is right. When opportunities arise, take them; don't obsess or over-worry about them being 100% right. Statistically, there is a far greater probability that your decision will be right than wrong.

A recent study[1] explored how many of a person's imagined calamities actually materialised. Eighty-five percent of what people worried about never happened. Out of the fifteen percent that did happen, seventy-nine percent of people discovered either they could handle the difficulty better than expected, or the difficulty taught them a lesson worth learning. This means that ninety-seven percent of what you worry over is not much more than a fearful mind punishing you with exaggerations and misperceptions.

Taking action is important to make things happen, but you must be open and flexible as to what, when and how, and avoid over-striving.

Turning intentions into reality

As a result of taking actions, things will start to happen for you as your intention starts to take form in the real world. It's important to notice and consciously celebrate all the small wins you have on the way to achieving your intentions.

Whilst over-analysis and excess thinking are to be avoided, it's important to get a sense that things are moving in the right direction, even if some of the pieces of the jigsaw puzzle are still missing.

If you are convinced you are moving in the wrong direction, use it as a learning opportunity. It's also worth revisiting the intention you set and checking if it's still right for you, or if it needs amending. Sometimes, by taking action and making things happen, you realise what you don't want, in turn helping you to become clearer about what you do want.

Things to remember in Step 4

In Step 3, once your intention felt right at a body and gut level, you started to walk the talk, embodying your intentions. Step 4 is about taking action that leads to your intentions taking shape in the real world. In reality, Steps 3 and 4 often merge or overlap. For clarity, I describe Step 4 as a distinct step. In the next few pages, you will find some tools and techniques that may help you with Step 4 of the IDEA framework.

Don't over-analyse

Your mind can really get in the way of achieving your intentions. It can over-intellectualise the process. It wants to know exactly the signs that demonstrate whether what you are doing is 'working' or not. It is always on the lookout for that 'proof' and a reason to feel better. There really isn't a foolproof way of determining if 'it's working', but it's possible to discover if you are on the right track, moving closer to what you want.

You might be FEELING BETTER. Whilst this may not be the answer you were hoping for, it's probably the biggest clue because it's difficult to achieve your intentions when feeling bad. When you are feeling good—or at least better—most of the time, you are aligning. It's then easier to notice and grasp all the things you want that will make you feel those same good feelings, and eventually lead you to the achievement of your intention. Feeling bad can slow or halt the process. Your state of mind and how you are feeling determine everything.

Maintaining momentum

You might notice that obstacles and difficulties arise. This is the part of the process that can really throw you and can feel disconcerting or downright unpleasant. In your impatience to achieve your intent, you realise you have taken the wrong turn or are on the wrong bus. Your expectations of how setting intentions was supposed to be, are different from how things really are at this moment. Obstacles and barriers arising is often a sign of forward movement. Stop worrying. It's OK. Overcoming obstacles helps you to see the 'lessons' you need to learn more quickly and be able to make the necessary shifts with less difficulty.

Allowing things to unfold

Some intentions may not fully manifest all at once; they unfold over time. Lots of nested intentions you did not even realise were nested intentions may start to manifest themselves.

For example, you set up a new business and set an intention to get fifty new customers. In reality, you might not get fifty in your first month. If you did, you would probably feel overwhelmed. Instead, you gain five clients here, three there, each the achievement of a smaller nested intention that leads to the achievement of your core intention—until eventually, you have fifty new customers. By thinking it's possible to get fifty new clients, your brain works hard behind the scene to help you notice and grasp opportunities to gain them. You notice opportunities you did not notice before.

Your intentions 'almost' take shape, but never feel fully realised. 'Almost intentions' can feel intensely frustrating and mess with your mind. You set an intention, only to find a situation arises that is not quite what you wanted. It has some good points, but there are some elements that don't sit quite well. You get offered your dream job working with your dream company, but the salary is terrible. Or, you get a job with a great salary but the tasks are not quite what you enjoy.

These things pop up to help you realise that you have a choice. They can help you solidify exactly what it is you want, and highlight when things don't fit the bill. There is never just one chance in life; the opportunities are infinite. Experiencing 'almost intentions' is often a sign you are starting to create your reality. The exciting bit is that you get to decide whether something that pops in is something you want or something you don't. You get to be discerning.

In summary, it can be frustrating to not know what is happening behind the scenes, and whether you are 'close' or not. It's normal to be mistrustful and to jump to negative conclusions. The truth is, you really can't know all that is happening, and the moment your intention is standing right on your doorstep, just waiting to walk in.

Feeling better, difficulties arising, nested intentions you did not know about cropping up, and too many 'almost intentions' are all signs things are moving in the direction you want them to. This is why it's so important to enjoy the journey, and find ways to feel good—right now.

You have set your intention and if it's right for you, it will come in some shape or form. It may look exactly like you pictured it or it may be something completely different but feels just as good, or even better.

If you discover that the intention you are working towards isn't quite right for you, take steps to refine it.

If after setting an intention and waiting for it to take shape, it starts to feel as if you don't want it enough, (or it isn't quite right for you, or you discover you want something subtly different), you need to refine your intention. Go back to Step 2 and try some of the exercises to help you refine your intent.

Knowing when to relax and allow it to happen when it happens

In one of my favourite jokes, a man is desperate for money, so prays to his God, "Oh lord, please help me to win the lottery". Each week, he prays the same, and each week he does not win. This continues for months until one day God replies to the man, "OK, I will help you win the lottery, but you have to meet me half way. You have to buy a lottery ticket!"

There is a fine line between sitting back and just expecting things to happen and trying too hard.

The act of sitting back and simply allowing things to be as they are or unfold in their own time is an alien concept for many. Interestingly, the act of trying too hard can activate your brain's threat response, and lead to you achieving less. You enter the zone of delusion, that dark place where you work really hard but achieve next to nothing.

When in the grip of the threat response, the primitive brain is in the driving seat which reduces your ability for big-picture thinking, creativity and doing things differently. The act of letting go of the outcome and simply allowing things to be as they are, switches down the threat response. When you are calm, you are better able to see the big picture and spot opportunities that may lead to the achievement of your intention.

Step 4 case study

Helen was shortlisted for the Director role. She invested all her free time and energy into preparing for her interview. She applied the principles she had learned from Amy Cuddy on the impact of body language on performance and others' perceptions of your capability. She studied the requirements of the role, and what had worked—and more importantly, not worked—for the previous Director in the role. She studied the power dynamics at play within the boardroom. She drafted a strategy and vision for the company moving forward. Helen was delighted to be offered the role.

In her first few months, she remembered the neurological importance of noticing and celebrating successes along the way. Things were moving in the right direction. Each month, she paid a little more off the mortgage, working towards being mortgage-free, now in four years instead of six. Her understanding of the politics at play in the boardroom helped her to unite and strengthen the board as a whole. Her achievements as a Board member surpassed her wildest dreams. Then, unexpectedly, the Chairman of the Board died very suddenly, and the Board was plunged into turmoil. A new Chairman was hastily appointed who did not see eye to eye with Helen. Helen's pleasure and sense of mastery in her new role started to dissolve and her confidence was eroded day by day.

After a few weeks of deep discomfort and disillusionment, she contacted me for some coaching. I helped her to revisit her intention to become the best leader she could be and to earn a sufficient income to live comfortably in her house and do the things in life she loved to do. She recognised that she now only had three and a half years left to pay off her mortgage. This job wasn't forever, just for a few short years.

She felt as if a weight had been lifted from her shoulders as she recognised that it was simply a small obstacle to be overcome in pursuit of a greater personal and organisational goal. I helped her identify some possible ways to help the Board work together in a more cohesive manner. At the next Board meeting, she helped the Board recognise the need for some external help. A consultant worked with the Board to help them assess the psychological sense of safety within the group and look at the dynamics from a brain-based perspective, so they could work together more effectively.

Three years later, Helen's mortgage was fully paid off. Her work in transforming employee motivation and organisational effectiveness via the introduction of purpose-based leadership gained her international recognition and a fair amount of press coverage.

As interest grew in her approach and experiences in purpose-based leadership, she spent an increasing amount of time helping other organisations to transform, something she loved to do. Originally, when she first set her intentions, Helen anticipated working less so she would have more time to do the things she loved. She realised that she now loved her job so much, she did not want to work less. She was already 'doing the things she loved'. Her newly-found financial freedom allowed her to make choices based on her wants rather than needs.

Helen had achieved her intentions. The intentions had unfolded in a way she couldn't have anticipated, and wouldn't have achieved with goals alone. This demonstrates the importance of identifying and distilling goals, then holding them lightly, allowing them to embed and unfold in unexpected ways. It also demonstrates the importance of taking action when opportunities arise rather than simply waiting for the intention to magically materialise.

Helen's way isn't the only way of working through Step 4 of the IDEA framework. To see alternatives, view the other case studies on my website.

Techniques to support action

When taking action towards your intentions, the need to 'hold your intentions lightly' and avoid 'over-striving'. Cannot be overemphasised.

The following tools may prove helpful in stage 4 of the IDEA process:

Seeing your intention taking form

To use a well-worn phrase, 'it's sometimes difficult to see the wood for the trees'. This tool may help you to more broadly monitor the ebb and flow of your intention journey.

1. Draw a timeline or diagram to graphically illustrate your journey towards your intention.

   a. Where are you now?

   b. Where do you want to be?

   c. How was your energy at each point on your timeline?

   d. When did progress accelerate or slow down?

   e. What was the cause? Personal? Technological?

2. This will help you to assess progress to date as well as drags and drivers.

Intention Action tool two: celebrating success

In the 1970s, BBC TV prison sitcom `Porridge', inmate Norman Stanley Fletcher constantly reminds his cell-mate Godber

'Small victories, Godber, small victories." Take a leaf out of Fletcher's book by noticing and celebrating the small victories of everyday life, as your intentions progress.

Doing so reinforces in your brain a sense of momentum and a feel-good factor. It links information, helping to reinforce your intention in your brain and leading to the release of feel-good hormones. Celebrating every small success may seem unnecessary or trivial but has a potent impact on your brain, accelerating your journey towards your intention.

Intention action tool three: Collaborate

If it feels right for you, look for opportunities to collaborate. Work with a select group of people to share ideas, overcome barriers and celebrate success. You might wish to form your own group, join the I-AM collective or seek coaching. More in Chapter 12.

Intention action tool four: Drawing a line under it

Sometimes, it's important to know when to stop. When you have been working on an intention for some time, ask yourself:

- Is it finished?
- Has it evolved or changed?
- Is it still unfolding?

If it has finished, let it go. Take some time to acknowledge this, and to gain a sense of completion, something you rarely notice in everyday life. If it has changed or evolved, let go of the old intention and move forward with the new, by distilling it (Step 2) if required. If it is still unfolding, let it continue to do so by letting it be.

Summary

When taking action towards a desired intention:

- Remember not to put yourself under pressure or agonise whether potential actions are right or wrong.

- Remember that statistically speaking, there is a far better chance of something good happening as a result of taking action, than of it going badly wrong. Imagined calamities rarely materialise.

- Intentions sometimes materialise in ways you cannot anticipate. Being too rigid in your expectations of how your intentions will unfold will restrict the opportunities open to you. This is why it's important to hold your intentions lightly.

- Additional resources and case studies that support this chapter are available from my website: www. intention-matters.com

References

1. Study presented in the book: Leahy, R.J. *The Worry Cure: Seven Steps to Stop Worry from Stopping You.* Harmony.Kindle Edition Nov. 2005

Part Three

Supercharging your intention

Chapter 10

Being mindful of your intention

"Mindfulness means being awake. It means knowing what you are doing."

– Jon Kabat-Zinn

In this chapter:

- ❧ *What is mindfulness?*

- ❧ *How to develop mindfulness*

- ❧ *How mindfulness aids the achievement of intention*

- ❧ *Mindful tools and techniques to help you work with intention*

Throughout this book, I have described how mindfulness provides a firm foundation for working with intention. At the outset of writing this book, I came to the realisation that intention = mindfulness + one. By this, I mean that if you have developed the basic ability to be mindful, intention takes your life to a whole new level. Over the last ten years, I have taught thousands of busy working professionals the basics of mindfulness and equipped them with the tools and techniques necessary to hardwire the mindful awareness into their brains.

In parallel with this, I co-designed and deliver Chartered Management Institute (CMI) recognised Workplace Mindfulness Training (WorkplaceMT)[1] and at the time of writing this, have taught over two hundred mindfulness trainers. Every day, I witness the transformative power of mindfulness. Mindfulness helps you to understand and manage your mind.

Over the last three years researching intention, I have seen many examples of people that work powerfully with intention, without knowing anything at all about mindfulness. You do not have to be mindful to work with intention but it gives you a distinct advantage. In this chapter, you will discover the basics of mindfulness, which may help you to supercharge your intentions.

What is mindfulness?

At its most basic level, mindfulness is a form of attentional training. By cultivating awareness of your thoughts, emotions and body-based responses (metacognition), your self-knowledge increases, enabling you to manage yourself better and make wiser decisions.

Many people think mindfulness is all about relaxation and emptying the mind. Nothing could be further from the truth. When practising mindfulness, the aim is not relaxation but focussing and maintaining attention. Many people say they feel relaxed after practising mindfulness. If this happens, it's a welcome by-product. Brain scans show that that the brain becomes more active when practising mindfulness, so rather than emptying the mind, you become more aware of everything happening around you.

Mindfulness is a self-management tool that helps you develop your ability to focus attention on the situation at hand, with the intention to observe the judgments you make, and choose how to respond appropriately. Developing this ability helps you to step away from autopilot or rote responses, observing with an open mind both context and different perspectives more clearly, and making smart decisions. Everyone has the capacity to be mindful, but like anything worthwhile, it takes time, effort, and practice.

Mindful intention

Mindfulness helps you to develop an enhanced awareness of what you are thinking, how you are feeling and what's going on in your body at any given moment. Every time you have a thought, it will trigger an emotion and a response in the body. Tension in the body may impact your emotional state and your behaviours. Every moment of every day, the interplay between thoughts, emotions and your physiology shapes your actions, often at an unconscious level. Developing metacognition allows you to break out of autopilot. Doing so allows you to make conscious decisions and respond more wisely. It helps you to minimise your primitive brain's over-the-top responses to life's challenges, helping you maintain an optimum state of mind for longer. This optimum mind state allows you to work towards your intention in a more mindful manner as detailed in the diagram below.

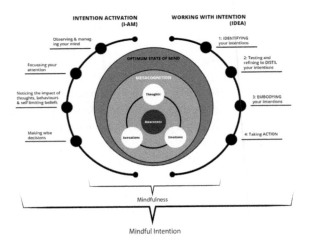

Figure 17: How mindfulness helps you to work with intention © 2019 Intentional Creations

Metacognition is the ability to observe what's going on in your mind. It enables you to become more aware of your automatic tendencies and responses. This awareness enables you to maintain an optimum mind state—to make decisions and act appropriately based on present-moment reality rather than being hijacked by strong emotions and impulses triggered by past experiences and predictions of the future, often leading to inappropriate actions and reactions.

An **optimum state of mind** can be described as a feeling of ease when you feel safe and secure, and your body and mind are functioning in their optimum states. In other words, this is when you are free from anxiety, anger, and fear, and are feeling secure, happy and comfortable with your surroundings. This state allows you to be the best you can and reach your full potential.

Mindful awareness involves being aware of aspects of the mind itself. You may recall that in Chapter 2, I described how the brain likes to automate tasks. It does this to help conserve energy and free up your energy-hungry neocortex to plan, dream, create or reflect. Whilst it is energy efficient, auto-pilot has a downside. Outdated and unhelpful mental processes may be running at a subconscious level. Mindful awareness helps you to recognise these and replace them with more appropriate patterns of thinking and behaviour.

The thing I love about mindfulness is its powerful transformative quality. In over thirty years of developing leaders, it's proved to be the most powerful tool I have ever worked with. It's a thousand times more powerful than any MBA program, psychometric tool, or management development fad I have ever encountered. By learning to observe the mind and its patterns, it enables you to make choices. It enables you to change, and no longer be a slave to the automatic patterns of your brain.

Key components of mindfulness training

There are many different versions of mindfulness training. Mindfulness training programs include:

- ❧ MBSR: Mindfulness-based Stress Reduction – originally developed for chronic pain sufferers.

- ❧ MBCT: Mindfulness-Based Cognitive Therapy – originally developed to reduce depression.

- ❧ WorkplaceMT: Workplace Mindfulness Training developed for busy working professionals to aid productivity and well-being.

All programs are broadly based on the same principles and consist of formal practice, psychological education and everyday informal practice.

Principles of mindfulness

A number of core principles underpin mindfulness training:

- ❧ **Intention, Attention and Attitude**. Mindfulness starts with setting an *intention* to develop skills so that you can act with full awareness. You pay *attention* to your thoughts, emotions and any physical sensations arising. You adopt an *attitude* of kindness, curiosity, openness and acceptance to what arises.

- ❧ **Accepting** and moving on from things rather than judging. When you make a judgement about something, you trigger a chain reaction of thoughts, emotions and physical reactions in the body that can make things worse than they actually are.

- ❧ **Being present** as opposed to mental time-travel – this enables you to make decisions based on present-moment facts rather than assumptions or predictions of the future.

- Stepping away from emotionally-driven **unconscious patterns of thinking and behaviour** that may not be serving you well.

- Being **open and curious** – approaching the world with childlike curiosity.

Psycho-educational themes of mindfulness training

- **Attention management** - Noticing mind-wandering and developing the capability to bring it back – improving your focus and attention.

- **The mind-body connection**. Every time you have a thought, it triggers an emotion and a bodily response. Mindfulness helps you to tune into emotionally-charged thoughts and the body's response. Instead of the body acting as an amplifier, it can become a sensitive emotional radar. This provides an early warning system alerting you to unhappiness, anxiety and stress almost before they arise.

- **Over-striving** - When things aren't working, many people push themselves harder and harder until they start to over-strive. Over-striving closes down the mind by narrowing the focus of perspective, inhibits creating thinking, and, ultimately, drives you to exhaustion.

- **Thoughts are not necessarily facts** - Observing thoughts as mental events. As humans, there is a tendency to treat thoughts as facts and use them as the basis for your decisions and actions. In reality, they are simply mental events created by your mind. Treating them as such, with the attitude that they are simply thoughts that may be right or wrong enables you to step back and make better decisions.

- ❧ **Approaching and exploring difficulties** or challenges you encounter in your life – you often waste more energy pushing away or avoiding difficulty than exploring, accepting or dealing with it.

- ❧ **Being kind to yourself** – it's impossible for the brain to operate in fight or flight ('something bad is about to happen, I need to protect myself') and be in a state of trust ('everything is ok, nothing is going to harm me') at the same time. The act of being kind to yourself or accepting your mistakes without getting frustrated or angry acts as a rapid off switch for the fight or flight response. This places your higher brain in the driving seat, allowing you to take conscious control of what's going on.

Formal meditation-based practice exercises

Many people make the mistake of thinking that reading a book or watching a video about mindfulness will make them mindful. This simply does not work. The capacity to be mindful is developed via time spent practising very specific meditation-based exercises. Research demonstrates that the benefits you experience increase in direct correlation to time spent practicing[2,3]. If you haven't much time to spare, the good news is that recent research[4] on workplace mindfulness suggests mindfulness can be developed with as few as ten to fifteen minutes of practice a day.

Whether you learn mindfulness via a face-to-face taught course, a book, an online course or via 1:1 coaching, you will be provided with recordings to guide you through the formal practices. In order for mindfulness training to be effective, it builds week on week, so the formal practice exercises should be practised in the right order. Each of the exercises should ideally be practised at least once a day for seven days before progressing to the next exercise. Workplace mindfulness training (WorkplaceMT) formal practice exercises are as follows:

- Week 1: Mindfulness of breath.

- Week 2: Body Scan.

- Week 3 Mindful movement + short mindfulness of breath and body.

- Week 4: Mindfulness of sounds and thoughts.

- Week 5: Approaching difficulty.

- Week 6: Cultivating kindness.

MBCT and MBSR mindfulness training follow a broadly similar pattern taught over an eight-week duration.

Informal 'everyday' mindfulness practice

Informal or 'everyday mindfulness' can be practised anywhere, anytime. Simply focus your full attention on what you are doing for a few minutes (longer if you have time). Informal opportunities to practice mindfulness might include:

- Showering mindfully - feeling the sensations of the water on your skin, the texture and scent of any shampoo or body wash you use.

- Drinking the first few sips (or the whole cup) of tea or coffee mindfully.

- Eating the first few bites (or whole plate) of food mindfully.

- Exercising mindfully: noticing when swimming, cycling, running or using repetitive gym equipment exactly how the body is feeling, and what is happening moment by moment – for a few seconds or minutes (or the whole time).

Mindfulness research & applications

Unlike many leadership and management training programs which have little or no independent research to demonstrate their effectiveness, mindfulness training is underpinned by over 3500 research studies published over a forty-year period.

Figure 18: Mindfulness timeline and research. © 2019 Intentional Creations

In recent years, researchers have turned their attention to the impact of mindfulness on a busy working population. To date, around 170 research papers have been published on the impact of mindfulness on employees. A recent meta-analysis[5] of research into mindfulness at work concluded there is robust evidence that mindfulness improves employee performance, relationships and well-being.

As well as studies measuring the outcomes of training, there are also studies that have attempted to map the changes in the brain after practising mindfulness for eight weeks or more. These studies suggest even modest practice times can fundamentally change the way in which the brain functions.

MRI brain scans show that as little as eight weeks of mindfulness practice shrink the amygdala (your brain's "fight or flight" centre). This primal region of the brain, associated with fear and emotion, is involved in the initiation of the body's response to stress. As the amygdala shrinks, the pre-frontal cortex—associated with higher-order brain functions such as awareness, concentration and decision-making—increases in size.

Mindfulness training changes the functional connectivity between these regions. Research suggests the connection between the amygdala and the rest of the brain gets weaker, while the connections between areas associated with attention and concentration get stronger.

The scale of these changes correlates with the number of hours of mindfulness practice, so you do need to work at it. Work by Adrienne Taren, a researcher studying mindfulness at the University of Pittsburgh, has concluded that "The picture we have is that mindfulness practice increases one's ability to recruit higher order, pre-frontal cortex regions in order to down-regulate lower-order brain activity." In laymen's terms, your primal responses to stress become superseded by more thoughtful ones.

Studies are also now beginning to show that mindfulness and meditation can have an impact at a genetic level[6]. There is a reduction in the shortening of teleomerases, the protective caps at the end of chromosomes, essentially meaning that age-related decline is reduced. This has also been seen in the structure of the brain. There is less age-related decline in the size of the hippocampus—the memory region—and less cortical thinning in the frontal lobe[7,8,9] in those who have regularly practised meditation. Practising mindfulness also improves your auto-immune system[10].

These neuroscientific investigations point to the way in which engaging and training your mind can change your brain for the better, in turn helping you work more effectively with intention.

How mindfulness supports the achievement of intention

When working with intention, you may need to override well-established habits and thought and behaviour patterns. Practising mindfulness helps you to recognise habits, changing them if they are no longer serving you well.

Using mindfulness to notice your habits

Habits are formed in the brain by repeating actions and/or

thoughts over and over again. As you do this, you form robust physical neural pathways in the brain, making it easier to repeat the thought or action in future. Habits are stored in the more primitive areas of the brain, meaning they can be repeated without conscious thought. The upside of this is that it's a tried and tested response that has worked in the past. It's also quick and energy efficient to repeat.

The downside is that responses that may have served you well in the past may not always be appropriate to present-moment situations. Despite this, especially when under pressure, your brain will default to old ways of thinking and doing things long before the conscious higher brain kicks in and you have the opportunity to question their appropriateness.

Practising mindfulness enhances your awareness of your unique patterns of behaviour and habits. This awareness is the first step towards replacing unhelpful habits with more appropriate ones via the power of neuroplasticity.

Using mindfulness to change your mindset

Changing your mindset can physically change your brain. In many ways, you create your own reality, so you become what you think. If you want to work effectively with intentions, you need to become more aware of your thoughts and their impact.

For example, you decide that you wish to gain a promotion and are invited to a job interview. If at an unconscious level you have self-limiting beliefs such as "I won't get it" or "I always screw up interviews," or "I haven't got enough experience," it will impact on the way you prepare for the interview. It will impact your presence when in the interview, and the way you answer questions. This, in turn, will impact on how your interviewers perceive you and their beliefs about your capability and desire to secure the promotion.

If you were mindful when invited to interview, you would be aware of your intention to gain a promotion. You would notice thoughts or emotions and/or tensions in the body. You could explore these playfully with an open mind, identifying what is triggering this response. You would become aware of thoughts of unworthiness, not feeling ready, or fear triggered by bad experiences at previous interviews. You would recognise that these thoughts are not necessarily facts. You would focus on present-moment facts such as 'I have been invited to the interview,' rather than time-travel to the past ('I made a mess of the interview last year') or future ('I will get nervous in the interview and look like an idiot').

In the interview, you would remember your intention to gain promotion. Mindfulness would help you to remain more present and calm, enabling you to consider and answer the questions better.

Mindfulness with intention points you directly to a radically-different way of living and relating. But it starts with some simple-sounding (but surprisingly challenging) practices, some of which are detailed later in this chapter.

How to develop mindfulness

Researchers believe it takes six to eight weeks to develop and embed a new skill in your brain. Developing mindfulness isn't instant either; it takes a little time and effort. The more you practice, the more embedded it becomes in your brain and the easier it becomes to be mindful in the face of life's challenges.

Mindfulness is developed through a combination of *psycho-education* (practical psychological models to help you to manage your mind), *formal practice* (very specific meditation-based exercises designed to help you to approach and explore present-moment reality rather than ignoring it, avoiding it, escaping it) and *informal everyday mindfulness* (paying some mindful attention to things you do every day).

To start to develop mindfulness, you could:

1. Attend a course. Find a trainer:

    a. MBSR or MBCT eight-week clinical model: http://bemindful.co.uk/learn-mindfulness

    b. WorkplaceMT six-week work-focussed mindfulness: http://workplacemt.com/trainers

2. Teach yourself mindfulness following guidance in a book and using pre-recorded MP3s:

    a. a. A general eight-week course is outlined in the book: Williams, M. and Penman, D. Mindfulness, a Practical Guide to Finding Peace in a Frantic World. Piatkus. 2011.

    b. b. A six-week course designed for professionals can be found in: Adams, J. Mindful Leadership for Dummies. John Wiley & Sons. 2016.Teach yourself mindfulness via an online course.

3. Be Mindful Online has been the focus of a robust academic study. It can be highly effective if you follow it as recommended by the course designers. Visit https://www.bemindfulonline.com/ for further details.

4. Learn mindfulness via 1:1 coaching. Executives, busy people and those with very specific needs often benefit from 1:1 coaching to develop mindfulness. Ideally, meetings should be face to face but can be facilitated via web-based meeting platforms such as Skype or GoToMeeting. Dr Tamara Russell and I have lots of experience in teaching mindfulness in this way. We can be contacted via the services pages of my website below. Some WorkplaceMT trainers also offer 1:1 coaching. Visit www.workplacemt.com for more details.

Mindful tools and techniques to help you work with intention

There are hundreds of ways that you could use mindfulness to help you to apply the four steps of the IDEA framework. For those readers who already have experience of mindfulness, here are a few ideas to get you started.

Should you wish to use them, mp3 recordings are available from my website.

Exercise 1: Tuning into your thoughts.

In Steps 1 and 2 of the IDEA framework, it can be helpful to identify any unconscious thoughts your brain associates with an intention you are working with. If you wish to use MP3 exercise IM3 to guide you.

1. Set an intention to practice and to be fully present with whatever arises.

2. Settle yourself into an upright chair in a position that embodies your intention to practice mindfulness (normal mindfulness postural set-up).

3. Spend five minutes undertaking a mini 'mindfulness of breath' exercise or body scan exercise.

4. Next, bring to mind your intention, and hold it lightly in your imagination.

5. Observe any thoughts that arise, however random.

   a. Avoid over-analysis or over-striving.

   b. Notice when your mind wanders, kindly and gently bringing it back.

6. After five minutes or so, let go of your intention

7. For the final minute or so, refocus your attention, bringing it back to sensations in the body. Avoid judgement—simply observe. When ready, open the eyes if they were still shut.

8. Note down the thoughts that arose.

9. Notice any themes that emerge. What does this tell you? Do you need to change or refine your intention in any way? Are there any self-limiting beliefs getting in the way?

Exercise 2: Using your body as a radar.

This is a great way of testing your intention at a gut level to surface any unconscious blocks to your intention. You could use it in IDEA Steps 1 and 2 to identify and distil intention. Equally, you could use it in Step 3 to test whether a potential opportunity that arises feels right. If you wish to use MP3 exercise IM4 to guide you.

1. Follow part 1-4 of Exercise 1 above.

2. Observe any sensations arising in the body. These might include tension, mild physical pain, a feeling of butterflies in your stomach, increased heartbeat or something else.

3. Unless the sensations are extremely intense, avoid trying to fix or change them. Simply observe your body's response when you are holding your intention in mind.

4. Follow parts 5, 6 & 8 of Exercise 1 above.

Exercise 3: Creating the space to see your intentions clearly

If you simply don't know what your intention is in Step 1 of the IDEA framework, this could be a great place to start. If you wish to use MP3 exercise IM4 to guide you.

1. Place a notepad and pen by your side. Settle yourself into a chair as detailed in Exercise 1, Step 2. Alternatively, lie down (but beware of the danger of falling asleep!)

2. Practice whichever mindfulness exercise you find most calming, ideally for around ten minutes.

Mindfulness of breath, body scan or mindfulness of sounds all work well here

3. Once you feel settled, you will be asking yourself some specific questions and waiting to see what happens. Some people simply like to ask questions, whereas others prefer to use imagery. If you like to use visualised imagery, you could try entering a historic setting, or a temple-like space. You could imagine a clinical setting with a workbench you use to examine things. You could go to a place you regard as safe or special in some way, such as a cave, a woodland setting, or a secluded area of nature. This is not mandatory, but some people find it helpful.

4. Ask yourself the question 'what do I most want?' Wait patiently to see if an answer arises. If it does, acknowledge it and repeat the question. See if something else comes up. Repeat until nothing further arises.

5. Ask yourself the question 'what do I most need?' Wait patiently to see if an answer arises. Repeat as above till nothing further arises.

6. When you are ready, prepare to leave your 'special place' if using one, and when you are ready, gently open your eyes if they were still shut. Spend a little time transitioning from your meditative state.

7. Note down all the answers you remember, underlining common themes or ideas that felt strongest, or that most excited you.

Exercise 4: Working with blocks and barriers

In Steps 3 and 4 of the IDEA framework, you may encounter blocks or barriers or a sense of frustration—because you may feel that nothing is happening. You may even feel you are not doing it correctly or that you've failed. This exercise may help you gain perspective and decide on a way forward. If you wish to use MP3 exercise IM6 to guide you.

1. Identify the difficulty you wish to work with. The difficulty might be a sense that nothing is happening. Maybe things not going to plan or as expected? Or, maybe you're getting what you intended but now feel that you don't want it?

    Whatever your block or barrier, set an intention for the exercise that you will explore it with an open mind, and accept whatever arises. *Note: it's important that you don't set an intention to 'solve the problem' or 'get a solution'. Doing so may trigger your threat response which, in turn, will inhibit your creativity and ability to see the bigger picture.* Be careful not to allow your inner gremlins tell you it won't work or that you'll be no good at it

2. Follow Steps 1 and 2 of Exercise 3 above

3. Bring to mind the barrier or challenge you are facing.

    a. If you are visual, spend some time exploring what it looks like.

    b. If you experience more of a 'felt sense' of the difficulty, explore any feelings that arise (emotional or physical).

    c. Notice any specific thoughts, emotions or physical sensations arising.

4. Repeat 3a-c above several times as you get closer and closer to your difficulty. Notice if anything changes, as it may or may not alter.

5. Let go of the difficulty and spend a few minutes focussing on the present-moment physical sensations arising as you breathe.

6. Redirect your attention to your body and get a sense of how your whole body feels at this moment. Open the eyes if they were still shut.

7. Use any insights gained to inform future actions, or decide on an alternative course of action.

Summary

- ❧ Mindfulness is a form of attentional training. By cultivating awareness of your thoughts, emotions and body-based responses (metacognition), your self-knowledge increases, enabling you to manage yourself better and make wiser decisions.

- ❧ Cultivating metacognition allows you to break out of autopilot. Doing so allows you to make conscious decisions and respond more wisely. This optimum mind state allows you to work towards your intention in a more mindful manner.

- ❧ When working with intention, you may need to override well-established habits and thought and behaviour patterns. Practising mindfulness helps you to recognise habits and change them if they are no longer serving you well.

✎ Additional resources and case studies that support this chapter are available from my website: www. intention-matters.com

References

1. WorkplaceMT is an evidence-informed approach to learning mindfulness which has been evaluated, researched and refined over four years. It started life in the Oxford Mindfulness Centre based on Mark Williams' and Danny Penman's book, 'Mindfulness: A practical guide to finding peace in a frantic world', (Piatkus, 2011) but has been adapted and refined to meet the challenges of the modern-day workplace. It's a robust, standardised mindfulness programme specifically developed for the workplace. Visit **http://workplacemt.com** for further information. The six-week training program is fully detailed in Mindful Leadership for Dummies (2016) by Juliet Adams.

2. Jha, Amishi., et al. (2015). *Minds "At Attention": Mindfulness Training Curbs Attentional Lapses in Military Cohorts* PLoS One.

3. Jha, Stanley, et al. (2016). *Practice is protective: mindfulness training promotes cognitive resilience in high-stress cohorts* Mindfulness 8(1) · January 2016

4. Mackenzie et al. (2006). *A brief mindfulness-based stress reduction intervention for nurses and nurses' aides* Applied Nursing Research ANR. 2006 May;19(2):105-9.

5. Good, Lyddy, Glomb et al. (2015). *Contemplating Mindfulness at Work: An Integrative Review* (2015).

Journal of Management, 42(1), 114-142.

6. Epel, Daubenmier, Moskowitz, Folkman, & Blackburn. (2009). *Can meditation slow rate of cellular ageing? Cognitive stress, mindfulness, and telomeres.* Annals of the New York Academy of Sciences. 2009 Aug;1172:34-53.

7. Lazar et al. (2005). *Meditation experience is associated with increased cortical thickness.* Neuroreport. 2005 Nov 28; 16(17): 1893–1897.

8. Britta Holzel et al. (2011). *Mindfulness practice leads to increases in regional brain gray matter density* . Psychiatry Res. 2011 Jan 30; 191(1): 36–43.

9. Desbordes et al. (2012). *Effects of Mindful-attention and Compassion Meditation Training on Amygdala Response to Emotional Stimuli in an Ordinary, Non-meditative State* (2012). Frountiers in Human Neuroscience 2012 Nov 1;6:292.

10. Davidson & Kabat-Zinn. (2004). *Alterations in brain and immune function produced by mindfulness meditation.* Psychosomatic Medicine. 2003 Jul-Aug;65(4):564-70.

Chapter 11

Overcoming common barriers

"The range of what we think and do is limited by what we fail to notice. And because we fail to notice that we fail to notice there is nothing we can do to change until we notice how failing to notice shapes our thoughts and deeds."

– R.D. Laing

In this chapter:

- *Limiting beliefs*

- *Rigid expectations that hold you back*

- *Unhelpful habits including procrastination and self-sabotage*

- *Managing your emotions*

- *Overcoming setbacks*

Working with intentions can be a highly rewarding experience. There are a few barriers that sometimes appear, creating an 'intention-action gap'.

In this chapter, I will outline a number of ways people get pulled off-track, and what you can look out for (and mitigate) so you can successfully work with intentions.

Immature manifestations of your intentions.

Have you set an intention and when it arrives, it does not turn out to be what you want? You may have experienced an immature manifestation of an intention. As the name suggests, it's an intention that is a juvenile version of what you want. It delivers part of what you want but is not fully formed or the full package. Maybe you have the intention to live in a beautiful cottage in the countryside. You find a house, but it turns out to have terrible damp, noisy neighbours, or to be underneath a busy flight path. Your intention delivered you a cottage in the country, but it does not deliver the idyllic country lifestyle you were anticipating.

The chances are that you set an intention to find a cottage with X number of bedrooms, in Y area for a budget of £Z. What you failed to specify was the condition of the cottage and the need for peace and tranquillity.

It's always a tricky balancing act when you set an intention. You need to be specific enough about the things that really matter but avoid restricting the formation of your intention by being overly specific. This is a judgement call and comes with experience. If you do encounter immature manifestations of your intentions, treat them as a learning opportunity, not a failure.

Limiting Beliefs

Your limiting beliefs are often unconscious. Limiting beliefs can potentially manifest in the following ways:

- Making excuses.

- Complaining about things.

- Indulging in negative thoughts.

- Indulging in unhelpful habits.

- Talking to yourself in limiting and unhelpful ways.

- Jumping to conclusions and/or making assumptions.

- Worrying about failure or about making mistakes.

- Worrying uncontrollably for no apparent reason.

- Procrastination.

- Perfectionism.

- Feeling a sense of resistance.

Let's say you have an intention to earn an extra £20,000 this financial year. However, as you're thinking about this goal, you start to feel a little uncertain and uncomfortable. This is precisely where you will find your limiting beliefs. These are the beliefs you need to bring into conscious awareness. You will find an exercise to help you surface your limiting beliefs in the final section of this chapter, 'overcoming barriers'.

Rigid expectations

As emphasised throughout this book, intentions require you to apply a softer and more flexible approach. You are working in the present moment with an aspiration for a different future. If you get too wedded to a particular outcome, you have essentially created a goal. Goals are more inflexible and less dynamic than intentions.

Overly rigid expectations give you tunnel vision and blind you to the myriad of possible avenues that might lead you to your destination.

Feeling an urge to plan is a very natural thing to want to do. The brain hates uncertainty and can treat it as a threat. Your brain will drive you to plan because this creates a sense of certainty and predictability that calm the brain and make it feel safe and in control. Use Steps 1 and 2 of the IDEA framework to check that your intention is really something you desire at a deep level and which you believe is possible.

It's good to have a plan to get you started, so, by all means, put some basic plans in place. The important thing is that you do something to get started and create some momentum. It does not matter if you end up going in the wrong direction for a little while, because this will then point you in the right direction. Hold the 'how to' part of your intention lightly and retain cognitive flexibility; this will allow you to notice and embrace opportunities you might not have discovered if you were excessively rigid at the outset.

If you are reading this now and have just discovered you are being hindered by overly rigid expectations—congratulations!

You have noticed! Now you are consciously aware of what's going on and can do something about it.

Letting go of expectations is something that improves with practice. It can be hard if you have strong "controlling" habits and is, of course, something that can be particularly difficult in the modern working environment where there is a strong emphasis on deliverables and certainty.

Remember: *"Holding on is believing that there's only a past; letting go is knowing that there's a future."*[1]

Letting go requires you to trust that you will be OK in that future moment, no matter what happens—whether your intention bears fruit or not.

Procrastination

Waiting for the time to be right is a common thought that might arise when you are considering what you really want and how you might like to get there. Sometimes, you want to wait until ALL the conditions are right for your big dream and plan to be initiated. After a while, you will realise that the time may never be fully "right" and in the meantime, life has passed you by. Now is the only moment you have, and even if there is only one small step you can take in the direction of your intention, this can be enough to get the ball rolling.

With intentions, the compass is set, but the end point is loose. What is one small thing you can do today that takes you one small step in the direction of what you want/intend?

Fear

Fear and doubt are common barriers, but they can be worked with, and over time, acknowledged and accepted as just part of the journey. It would be unusual if they weren't there—especially if you are going after something that is really meaningful—but you don't need to let them take control or overwhelm you.

When experiencing fear, you may notice:

- ๑ Increased heart rate

- ๑ Sweating

- ๑ Jelly legs

- ๑ Feeling sick/nausea

- ๑ Throat dry or tight

- ๑ Muscles tightening and the body bracing

- ๑ Posture becoming defensive (hunched over, going into the foetal position)

- ๑ Your body freezes and you feel unable to move.

Set a nested intention to be courageous as you work with intentions. This will help you to notice more promptly when fear is holding you back. Don't let fear be the basis of your decisions.

Sunk-cost bias

Have you ever bought a stunning pair of designer shoes, and worn them despite the fact they really hurt your feet—simply because you felt the need to get your money's worth? Have you ever held onto something you bought but don't use or particularly like simply because it was expensive? Have you ever kept reading a book or watching a film right to the end, despite the fact you were not enjoying it? Have you remained in a business partnership or stuck to a business strategy primarily because you'd heavily invested in it—when it was clearly not working?

If you answered yes to any of the above, you've experienced a "sunk-cost bias." Sunk cost bias is the tendency to continue investing in a losing proposition because of what it's already cost you. Humans are all innately loss-averse. Who wants to take a loss or admit they wasted money, time or energy that could have been better spent?

When working with intention, particularly in stages 3 and 4 of the IDEA framework, watch out for sunk-cost bias. If something isn't working, or it's no longer what you want or need, let it go, change your direction or refine your intention.

Self-sabotage

Self-sabotage is often triggered by a fear of getting what you want. Self-sabotaging behaviour creates problems in your life and interferes with the achievement of your intentions. Common self-sabotaging behaviours include procrastination, self-medication with drugs or alcohol, anger, comfort eating, and forms of self-injury such as cutting. These acts may seem helpful in the moment, but they ultimately undermine your efforts, especially when you engage in them repeatedly.

People aren't always aware of their own self-sabotage, or the damage it is causing, because the effects of their behaviour may not show up for some time.

When working with intention, some people experience self-sabotage. At some level, they feel their success is unwarranted. Humans may even experience fear of their own power—fear that they might really be OK, fear of succeeding.

For you, these fears may be deeply hidden, or you may be painfully aware of them. Keep a look out for your "what if" inner voice. It might be whispering to you:

- ❧ What if I succeed?
- ❧ What if I don't succeed?
- ❧ What if I get it wrong?
- ❧ What if I can't cope?

Sometimes, your own 'what if' voice can be helpful, allowing you to imagine a future and make a rich representation in your mind of how things might look or feel once the intentions happen. At other times, the picture of success in the future comes with less positive emotions. For some, success may bring its own worries and fears. Getting a good sense of your 'what if's' will help you to identify, understand and remove any blockages.

Tools and techniques to help you to overcome barriers

In the next few pages, you will find some tools and techniques designed to overcome barriers

Tool 1: Stop procrastinating

Try one or more of these to shake yourself out of procrastination and into action.

1. Set a timer and get started on the task for just fifteen or twenty minutes. Commit to doing twenty minutes and even if you just sit there looking at a blank screen, this is OK. You have started. What often happens is that setting a shorter time limit (rather than the larger task of "I have to do it all now") breaks the task down a bit and makes it feel more manageable. Once you get going, you will find that you can probably keep going and do a bit more, you may even get it done.

2. Sometimes, an intention can seem overwhelming and procrastination kicks in, inhibiting forward motion. Try to find one small thing you can do right now, or today, that will take you in the direction you want to go. Make this action with full awareness and direction (of your intentions). It does not matter if it's only a tiny thing; you are moving in the direction of your intention. Doing this with awareness makes it even stronger. You are building up the intention muscle a little bit at a time. You are on the right track, even if the step is only a tiny shuffle forwards.

3. If you try techniques 1 and 2 (above) and get nowhere, take a moment to pause and explore in your mind and body... what is really getting in the way?

Tool 2: Changing the way you behave

How can you really ground your intentions? The knowledge, skills, and confidence framework is one that has been shown by research to support people to change behaviours. It's used in health research to help people get over the intention-action gap.

Clients working with my friend and collaborator in this work— Dr Tamara Russell—found the following to be a helpful checklist to see what's needed to progress, and who or what can help when you are feeling stuck.

1. **Knowledge** - do you have the right technical knowledge to execute your intentions? If not, who can help or where do you need to do some more desk or other research?

2. **Skills** – do you have the skills to execute the sub-goals or steps required to take you forwards? Be realistic about your skills gaps. Seek training where necessary. Think about who you might recruit to help you.

3. **Confidence** (self-efficacy) – How confident are you that you will achieve what you have set out to do? Be realistic about this. Its OK (and natural) to have doubts. Own them in a mindful way, non-judgmentally, with curiosity, without reacting and being too hard on yourself.

When working with Step 3 above, Tamara favours a solution-focused approach, to explore confidence in more detail:

❧   Thinking about your intention with real honesty, how

confident are you that you will achieve what you have set out to do?

- ❧ Rate your score on a scale of 0 (not at all confident) to 10 (absolutely certain).

- ❧ Ask yourself "If I woke up tomorrow and the project were all I had dreamed it to be, what would be happening? What would it look like? What would I be doing? Feeling? Experiencing?"

Having acknowledged that there may be some psychological barriers lingering in relation to this intention, once again look at the scores you assigned on the rating scale. If you gave a score of 7/10—what would move that score right from a seven to an eight? Reflect on this.

Similarly, what would move the rating one point to the left? What would make the seven a six? Reflect on this.

Being aware of fears, judgements and self-limiting beliefs gives you choices. It can help you to regain your sense of control and give you a sense of relief. You don't have to remove doubt entirely, just know that it is there.

Tool 3: Removing limiting beliefs

If you set an intention but afterwards, when you are thinking about it, you start to feel a little uncertain and uncomfortable, limiting beliefs may be getting in the way. In order to progress, you need to bring them into conscious awareness. You can do so by asking yourself the following questions:

? What resistance am I feeling inside while I think about achieving this goal?

? Why can't I overcome certain challenges to achieve my goal? What is holding me back?

? What specifically is getting in the way?

? What unhelpful habits am I indulging in?

? How am I thinking about this situation?

? What am I saying or doing to myself that is holding me back?

? What excuses do I tend to indulge in? What do these excuses mean? Why do I make them?

? Why do I think this is hard or too difficult? What is stopping me? Why?

? What kind of things do I tend to complain about, or blame others for?

? Do I potentially have any psychological rules that are preventing me from moving forward?

? What negative and pessimistic thoughts do I tend to indulge in while pursuing this goal?

? What assumptions or conclusions am I making about my inability to achieve this goal?

? Do I have any global beliefs that might be holding me back?

? What do I expect should happen? What usually ends up happening? Why is there a discrepancy here?

? Are my standards too low? Why? Maybe, I should set the bar higher?

> ? Do I have any values in conflict with my goals? What do I believe about these values?
>
> ? How am I labelling myself and/or describing myself as I work toward this goal? How could this be causing problems?
>
> ? What stories do I tell myself about what I should or shouldn't be doing, and about what should or shouldn't happen? How is this of significance?

Having taken the time to reflect on these questions, it's important that you specify correctly what kind of limiting beliefs are currently holding you back. Ask yourself:

> ? What insights do the answers to these questions provide about my limiting beliefs?
>
> ? What specific limiting beliefs are holding me back right now?
>
> ? How are these limiting beliefs preventing me from achieving my desired goals and objectives?
>
> ? How are these limiting beliefs denying me the opportunity to become the person I want to be?

Remember that your limiting beliefs are assumptions you make about reality that aren't true in your particular situation. They aren't helpful, and they certainly don't serve you or the goals you want to achieve.]

Tool 4: Working with fear

Fear of being judged, of getting it wrong, of being humiliated, rejected, or abandoned can all have the intensity of the more primitive fears of death, injury etc. If fear is stopping you, you and only you can stop the fear. When experiencing fear, try one or more of the following.

Familiarise yourself with your fears

The best way to work with this is to become familiar with what it feels like to be fearful. Get to know the pattern of fear in the body.

Pause for a minute now to consider the last time you were really afraid.

a. What was the situation? What was happening? Were you in physical or psychological danger?

b. Allow yourself time to generate a rich memory of the situation and then tune into the body; what do you feel?

c. When you experience fear, what do you notice in the heart region? Here there are often more subtle sensations. Is the heart opening or closing? Is there a sense of expansion or contraction?

Set an intention to be courageous

Being courageous can help you overcome fear.

Bring to mind a role-model or someone in your life you know to be courageous. Keep this person in mind when you feel afraid or uncertain. Hear their voice, picture their face. What would they say to you at this moment?

Feel the fear and do it anyway

Do one small thing that scares you every day. When you deliberately put yourself into a fearful physical situation, observe the mind and body and really observe your unique patterns of thinking and behaviour.

Be mindful of your fears

Mindfulness can really help you to work differently when you encounter strong emotions like fear. Regular mindfulness practice can help you to see more clearly how, when and why these mental patterns are triggered and play out. Knowing them more thoroughly means you have more power over them. They may still emerge and arise, but you will be less pulled by them and more able to disengage and come back.

Tool 5: working through frustrations

a) In moments of frustration, try to really tune into the tone of the inner voice that you are experiencing at this moment.

b) Notice what your inner voice is saying. It might be saying "That's not what I was planning" or "this is going nowhere" or "It just isn't happening".

c) How many different tones of voice can you use to make this sound?

d) Try changing the emotional underpinnings of these inner voice messages; change the patterns of stress and intonation. How does this change things? What do you notice?

Tool 6: Maintaining your energy and focus

A recent Harvard Research[2] study suggests that for almost half of your working day, your mind may be wandering. Attention Management has been deemed to be one of the most critical skills of the twenty-first century. With so many electronic distractions how you manage your energy is vital, now more than ever.

In the same way as working on an important project, working with intention requires you to keep your energy tank full. Your energy tank needs to be recharged and refilled regularly. To check your energy level, this exercise, lifted from mindfulness training, can be very valuable.

1. List the main activities of your day.

2. Mark them with an 'N' if they nourish you or a 'D' if they deplete or drain you of energy

3. Take a look at the balance of your list. How many N's are there? D's?

4. If there are more 'D' than 'N', how will you alter the balance? What pleasurable activities will you add back into your life?

Summary

Working with intentions can be exciting and life-changing but a number of things can pull you off track. These may include immature manifestations of intentions, limiting beliefs, rigid expectations, procrastination, fear, sunk-cost bias and self-sabotage.

> ✎ Stop procrastinating by setting a timer for twenty

minutes and doing something, however small.

- ✎ Change the way you behave by exploring your values, self-labelling and stories you tell yourself.

- ✎ Remove self-limiting beliefs by surfacing them and reflecting.

- ✎ Work with fear by getting to know them, being courageous and doing something that scares you whenever you can.

- ✎ Work through frustrations by tuning into the tone of your inner voice and changing the emotional underpinnings.

- ✎ Maintain energy and focus by balancing both nourishing and depleting activities.

- ✎ Additional resources and case studies that support this chapter are available from my website: www.intention-matters.com

Being mindful of your thoughts, emotions and physical responses will help you to recognise and—with time and patience—overcome any barriers you face.

References

1. Daphne Rose Kingma
2. Killingsworth and Gilbert (2010). *A wandering mind is an unhappy mind.* Science. 2010 Nov 12;330(6006):932.

Chapter 12:

Next steps

"You've got to know what you want. This is central to acting on your intentions. When you know what you want, you realize that all there is left then is time management. You'll manage your time to achieve your objectives because you clearly know what you're trying to achieve in your life."

– Hunter Doherty "Patch" Adams, physician, social activist, founder of the Gesundheit! Institute, and author.

In this chapter:

- ❧ *Training and support*
- ❧ *Additional information and resources*
- ❧ *Further reading*

Intention Matters has been designed as a self-help book and is designed to equip you with everything you need to change your life with intention.

If you feel you would like to develop further or want some help and support, the next few pages may be of assistance.

Training to help you work with intention

I offer one-day and weekend training courses to help you understand and immerse yourself in setting and working with intentions. Details of this are posted on my Intention-matters website.

The I-AM collective

The I-AM collective is a lively online group set up to encourage collaboration and sharing of ideas.

It's a fun, flexible and accessible option for those who would like further support on their intention journey. Members share their successes and support each other to overcome any barriers they encounter.

The I-AM collective provides ongoing collaboration and information-sharing for those who have attended my workshops or purchased my books. For a nominal monthly fee, subscribers will have free access to additional resources, tools, and information. In addition, they can meet with others online via monthly live web meets hosted by the author and key collaborators in this book. Each web gathering will include expert input on specific aspects of working with intention and allow time for individual Q&A.

More information is available on my website.

One-to-one coaching

If you feel you would benefit from one to one coaching and/ or mentoring with me—Juliet Adams—or Dr Tamara Russell, please contact us via my intention-matters website. If we are unable to offer this due to other commitments, we will happily suggest some alternatives to help you to move forwards.

Form your own group

The aim of this book is to give you the confidence and knowledge to work with intention. If you wish to collaborate with others to share ideas and support each other, why not form your own group? You can meet online or face to face.

Meeting on a regular basis with others working with intention will help you to keep motivated. As the group organiser, you will benefit from the experience and wisdom of others. If you do set up a group, we would love to hear how you get on. Do share your success stories by emailing me via the contact page of my website below.

Additional tools and resources

Case studies

In part 2 of this book, I mentioned a number of case studies that illustrate different ways to apply and work with the IDEA framework. The case studies can be downloaded free of charge from my website.

Additional tools to work with Steps 1-4 of the IDEA framework

I have developed additional tools to help you to apply the IDEA framework. These are available to I-AM Collective subscribers.

Additional tools to help you overcome barriers and setbacks

We have developed some additional tools to help you to overcome barriers and setbacks. These are available to I-AM Collective subscribers.

Further reading

Research into the neuroscience of intention:

- ❧ Anscombe, G.E.M. Intention. Harvard University Press; 2nd edition, 2000).

- ❧ Benjamin Libet's work on the neuroscience of free will. Libet, Benjamin (1985). Unconscious cerebral initiative and the role of conscious will in voluntary action. The Behavioral and Brain Sciences. 8 (4): 529–566. doi:10.1017/s0140525x00044903. Retrieved 18

December 2013

- Damasio, Antonio. (2006). *Descartes' Error: Emotion, Reason and the Human Brain.* Vintage, 2006.

- M. Bratman. (1987). *Intention, plans, and practical reason.* Cambridge, MA: Harvard University Press.

- McTaggart, Lynne. (2008). *The Intention Experiment.* (2007). Harper Element

- Mele, A. *Effective intentions: The power of conscious will..* New York, NY: Oxford University Press, 2009.

- Pacherie, Elisabeth. (2000). *The content of intention.* Mind and Language 15 (4):400-432 (2000)

- Schmidt, S. (2012). *Can we help just by good intentions? A meta-analysis of experiments on distant intention effects.* Journal of Alternative Complimentary Medicine. 2012 Jun;18(6):529-33. doi: 10.1089/acm.2011.0321.

- Slors, M. (2015). *Conscious intending as self-programming.* Philosophical Psychology, 28 (1), 94-113.

Books on Mindfulness

- Adams, J. (2016). Mindful Leadership for Dummies. John Wiley & Sons.

- Russell, T. (2017). What Is Mindfulness? Watkins Publishing.

- Williams, M. and Penman, D. (2011). Mindfulness, a Practical Guide to Finding Peace in a Frantic World. Piatkus.

What Did You Think of Intention Matters?

I would value your feedback....

First of all, thank you for purchasing **Intention Matters**. I know you could have picked any number of books to read, but you picked this book and, for that, I am extremely grateful.

I hope that it added value and quality to your everyday life. If so, it would be really nice if you could share this book with your friends and family by posting to Facebook, Instagram, and Twitter; #intention-matters-book.

If you enjoyed this book and found some benefit in reading this, I'd like to hear from you and hope that you could take some time to post a review on Amazon. Your feedback and support will help me to greatly improve my writing craft for future projects and make this book even better.

I want you, the reader, to know that your review is very important and so if you'd like to leave a review, all you have to do is click here and away you go.

I wish you all the best in your future success!

Glossary of terms

Acceptance
A term used in mindfulness. Allowing things to be as they are in this moment without trying to change them.

Action (A)
A term used in the I-AM model – Taking action to make an intention happen.

Activating Will (AW)
A term used in the I-AM model – Cognitive process in the brain, involving the desire to act and a sense of responsibility for your actions. Involves the anterior cingulate cortex (responsible for motivation and planning), and precuneus cortex, an area associated with agency.

Allocating Attention (AA)
A term used in the I-AM model – Cognitive process in the brain involving prefrontal cortex and parietal cortex.

Amygdala
Part of the brain - an almond-shaped set of neurons located deep in the brain's medial temporal lobe. Plays a key role in the processing of emotions.

Approach mode of mind
Mindfulness helps you cultivate an approach mode of mind, actively exploring it with openness and curiosity – the opposite of avoidance (doing something to avoid something bad happening. Approach mode can improve creativity by 50%.

Attentional Network	Areas of the brain responsible for directing and sustaining attention. The prefrontal cortex is thought to control the brain's attention.
Autopilot	A term used in mindfulness to describe how much of your life is conducted on autopilot – without your conscious control. Autopilot responses can be inappropriate to the situation.
Basal ganglia	Part of the brain associated with movement, learning, habit learning, cognition, and emotion.
Belief (B)	A core component of intention (see intention below). Part of the I-AM model - an acceptance that an intention will happen or is possible.
Bias	An inclination or prejudice.
Brain	Physical hardware that occupies space in your skull. It transmits information via chemical impulses and gathers information via the five senses, links it to existing information stored in the brain. Stores and retrieves information.
Brain stem	The brain stem controls the flow of messages between the brain and the rest of the body, and it also controls basic body functions such as breathing, swallowing, heart rate, blood pressure, consciousness, and awakeness.
Cerebral cortex	Part of the brain responsible for thinking, perceiving, producing and understanding language, and information processing.

Cognitive Processes (CP)	Part of the I-AM model. Refers to a range of processes involving different areas of the brain that contribute to the achievement of an intention. Key cognitive processes include sensation, perception, attention, memory, and thought.
Core intention	Core intentions have the capacity to be life-changing. They are smaller in scale than mega intentions.
Day-changing intention	A micro intention that could change the course of your day.
Deep, Sincere Desire (DSD)	Part of the I-AM model, and the definition of intention (see below). A heartfelt as opposed to superficial desire for something to happen.
Default Mode Network (DMN)	A network within the brain that is most active when the brain is at rest. It is also active when the individual is thinking about others, thinking about themselves, remembering the past, and planning for the future.
Distal	Distal intentions are further away in time and may take longer to achieve. Core and mega intentions are examples.
Dopamine	An important chemical messenger in the brain. Involved in reward, desire, motivation, memory, attention, learning, and emotional responses.
Embodying	Part of the IDEA framework (see below). In Step 3 of the framework, you start to embed the intention into your life, thereby embodying it.

Functional magnetic resonance imaging	Sometimes called or functional MRI (fMRI) Brain-scanning technology that measures brain activity by detecting changes associated with blood flow.
Goals	Goals are different from intentions. They are future focussed, narrow, a destination or specific achievement, usually short-term, fixed and logical.
Gut instinct	In your gut is a network of neurones. The network is so extensive, scientists have nicknamed it 'the little brain'. The little brain influences your emotions and determines your mental state. Gut instinct taps into your unconscious mental state, sending information from the gut to the brain, to inform decisions.
Habits	A routine or behaviour that is repeated regularly and tends to occur subconsciously.
Happening (H)	Part of the I-AM model. Refers to an intention becoming a reality.
I-AM model	Intention Activation Model – explains how the mind tasks the brain, tasking the body to make things happen in the outside world.
IDEA Framework	A four-step framework designed to help you work with intention. Step 1: Identity, 2: Distil or refine, 3: Embody and embed, 4: Take action.
Immature manifestation of an intention	Setting an intention delivering exactly what you asked for, but which isn't what you actually need or want. The intention emerges into your life in an immature state in need of further refinement.

Intention	Defined in this book as 'A deep sincere desire, underpinned by a belief that it is possible'. Intention forms (in order of scale) include micro, nested, core, and mega.
Life-changing intention	Core intentions and mega intentions. The latter has the potential to change the world.
Limiting beliefs	Beliefs constraining you in some way. They are often about you and your self-identity. They may also be about other people and the world in general.
Mega intention	Huge potentially world-changing intentions. May take a lifetime to achieve.
Metacognition	An awareness and understanding of your thought processes. The ability to observe what's going on in your mind.
Micro Intention	Day or instant moment-changing intentions. smaller in scale and duration than nested or core intentions.
Mind	Instructs the brain. It's not a physical object. It turns chemical/electrical impulses into mental experiences (images or thought). It uses the information gathered to enable you to become consciously aware of the world and your experiences, thoughts and feelings.
Mind-body connection	Your mind is influenced by how your body feels, and your body is influenced by your mind. Communication between the two is both top-down and bottom-up.

Instant intention	In this book, a micro intention is described as 'a day-changing or instant, moment-changing intention'.
Nested intentions	Intentions that may contribute to the achievement of a core or mega intention.
Neurones	Also called neurons or nerve cells - the cells in your brain responsible for receiving sensory input from the external world, for sending motor commands to your muscles, and for transforming and relaying the electrical signals at every step in between.
Neuroplasticity	The brain's ability to reorganise itself by forming new neural connections throughout life. The things we say or think most often form stronger physical connections in the brain.
Nucleus Accumbens	Part of the brain playing a central role in the reward circuit. Its operation is based chiefly on two essentials: dopamine and serotonin.
Open monitoring	In mindfulness meditation, attentional focus may be narrow (focussed on one point) or wide – a spacious awareness of everything happening around you. This is sometimes called 'open monitoring'.
Motor representation (MR)	Occurs in the brain - the mental precursor of action - normally conscious.

Optimum state of mind	In the mindful intention model, an 'optimum state of mind' is one where the brain feels safe and secure. In this state, you can more readily tap into your higher-brain thinking capacity and have more conscious control.
Over-striving	Placing yourself under excessive pressure in pursuit of a goal or intention. Excessive pressure dramatically reduces your creativity, ability to make good decisions, and performance overall.
Proximal	Proximal intentions are close in time – micro intentions are examples of this.
Rationality	The quality or state of being rational.
Reward system	The reward system is a collection of brain structures responsible for reward-related cognition, including positive reinforcement, your 'wants', and 'likes'.
Right/left hemisphere	The brain consists of two cerebral hemispheres separated by a groove. The brain is thus divided into left and right cerebral hemispheres. Each has an outer layer of grey matter, supported by an inner layer of white matter.
Rituals	A ceremony consisting of a series of actions performed according to a prescribed order. Some people create their own rituals to help them to embed their intentions into their brains.
Self-sabotage	Behaviour creating problems in life and interfering with goals and intentions. May include procrastination, self-medication with drugs or alcohol, comfort eating.

Serotonin
: An important chemical messenger in the brain. Effects include a sense of a need being met and inhibition of impulses.

Subconscious brain
: A vast memory bank that stores your beliefs, memories and life experiences. This information affects your behaviour and actions in different situations.

Sunk-cost bias
: A tendency for people to irrationally follow through on an activity/project not meeting their expectations, due to the time and/or money already invested in it.

Thalamus
: An area of the brain involved in sensory and motor signal relay and the regulation of consciousness and sleep.

Three brain systems
: It can be helpful to think of the brain as having three key systems. At the base of the brain is the '**brain stem**' (basic survival functions). Above this can be found the '**Limbic system**' (emotional responses). On top is the '**neocortex',** (processes information, works to achieve tasks, goals and conscious intentions.

Working memory
: The part of short-term memory in your brain concerned with immediate conscious perceptual and linguistic processing.